Introduction to Academic English Writing

Introduction to Academic English Writing

By

BRENDAN M. HOWE & HEATHER A. WILLOUGHBY

Ewha Womans University Press

Introduction to Academic English Writing
By BRENDAN M. HOWE & HEATHER A. WILLOUGHBY

First published 21 November, 2005
Second printing 19 April, 2010
Published by Ewha Womans University Press
11-1 Daehyun-dong, Seodaemun-gu, Seoul, Korea 120-750
Tel. (82-2)3277-3164, 362-6076
Fax. (82-2)312-4312
E-mail: press@ewha.ac.kr
Online Bookstore: www.ewhapress.com

price: 10,000 won

ISBN 978-89-7300-647-2 93740

Foreword

This book is the third volume of the international studies series planned by the Specialization Committee on International Studies of Ewha Womans University. This is an academic English writing book written by academics with an inter-disciplinary and international background, who draw on many years of experience of teaching university courses in the social sciences and humanities, identifying key common failings and addressing them with simple rules, guidelines and models. It covers a number of practical components of academic English writing. That is to say, it deals with a far more formal approach to written English than might be employed on a day-to-day basis in letters and e-mails, sending text messages on our mobile phones, or instant messaging on our computers.

However, formal or structured does not necessarily mean unimaginative or dry. Done well, academic English writing has its own form of elegance and style. A well-crafted submission can make the difference between winning and losing a debate, or between a higher and lower grade. The purpose of academic English is to communicate your ideas as effectively as possible. Effectively means clearly, convincingly, concisely and yet comprehensively. Information and arguments must not only be reported accurately and efficiently, but also in a compelling way that paints you the author in the best light.

This volume aims to provide a service to non-native English speaking students (although many native speakers could also find useful material within its pages), who are either applying to, or have been accepted into a course in which the teaching medium is English.

It contains a handy reference section (Chapter 2) on some of the most important elements of grammar, and common grammatical mistakes encountered when non-native English speakers embark upon academic English writing projects. However, it is not a grammar book. It is a practical self-help book designed to teach the student the fundamental rules for the construction of sentences, paragraphs, essays and larger research projects, while at the same time avoiding some of the pitfalls (such as plagiarism) that often serve to undermine written submissions.

I am very glad that this book is the third publication of the Jang-Hee Yoo Series on International Studies, named for Jang-Hee Yoo, Vice President, External Affairs of Ewha Womans University, founding Dean of the Graduate School of International Studies and the Division of International Studies, and a great champion of international studies in Korea.

Brendan Howe, Series Editor
Director, International Studies Program
Ewha GSIS

Contents

List of Contributors

Dr. Brendan Howe is an Assistant Professor of Diplomacy and Security at Ewha Division of International Studies as well as faculty advisor to the university debating teams. He has written extensively on many philosophical and political issues, and also has a background in academic book publishing. He has taught college students in seven countries on three continents (the United States, the United Kingdom, the Republic of Ireland, the Peoples' Republic of China, the Republic of Korea, Malaysia, and Singapore) and from many other nationalities. In addition to his political teaching, Dr. Howe teaches academic English courses at both the high school and college level.

Dr. Heather A. Willoughby is an Assistant Professor in the Division of International Studies at Ewha Womans University. Although her Ph.D. is in ethnomusicology, she has comprehensive training in social and cultural anthropology, and Korean studies, with broad interests in East Asian history, society, culture, politics, music, literature, and religion. Dr. Willoughby has been a musician, poet, and writer most of her life; publishing both academic and non-academic works. This, however, is her first, and promises to be her last foray into writing about the subject of grammar. Her best friend, who has a Ph.D. in English Literature, was once asked whether or not she pursued the study of syntax or only creative writing, to which she responded, "None grammar." And that says it all!

Jacob Reidhead is currently studying in a masters program at Korea University. He was the recipient of a National Security Education Program Undergraduate Scholarship and a National Language Initiative Graduate Fellowship, both for study of the Korean language. Over the past five years Jacob has translated and edited Korean academic writing in a variety of disciplines including biochemistry, information security, women's studies, and law.

Chapter 1 Introduction

1.1 Defining academic English writing

It may be easiest to explain the concept of this book by saying what academic English is not. It is not the kind of creative writing we are familiar with from novels, plays or poems. It is also not the kind of conversational English or casual English that we might employ on a day-to-day basis when writing letters and e-mails, sending SMS (short message service) texts on our mobile phones, or instant messaging on our computers. Academic English employs far less imagery than the former and is far more structured than the latter. In many ways academic English allows us less freedom to express ourselves as writers.

There are many rules we must follow lest our work suffer when others evaluate it. We must avoid the elaborate metaphors and similes of creative writing, and the abbreviations, slang, casual language, and shortcuts we use when communicating with our friends. In our many years of teaching students in different countries with different levels of English expertise, we have found on many occasions that students easily get confused between these types of written English, either resorting to inappropriate elaboration, or using inexact terms and structures.

However, while academic English writing may not have the beauty of creative writing or the brevity of memos, texts, or e-mails, done well, it has its own form of elegance and style. A well-crafted submission can make the difference between winning and losing a debate, or between a higher and lower grade. The purpose of academic English is to communicate your ideas as effectively as possible. By effectively we mean clearly, convincingly, concisely and yet comprehensively. Information and arguments must not only be reported accurately and efficiently, but also in a compelling way that paints you, the author, in the best light.

Think of the reader of your piece of academic English writing as your audience. It is your job to win the audience over to your side. This does not necessarily mean that the reader must leave agreeing with everything you have said. Rather, it means that the reader must upon completion be left with a sense of respect for your mastery of the rules and structures of academic English. A bad argument is still a bad argument, and is unlikely to win anybody over, even if well crafted. However, a good argument badly written can end up being wasted on the audience, either because she does not understand what is being said, or because poor style has undermined good content leading to a poor overall impression. With equal content, a better piece of writing will gain higher marks than a less well-crafted piece, and may even rank higher than a piece with superior content.

1.2 Using academic English

With the growth in popularity of high school educational qualifications such as the International Baccalaureate, larger numbers of students are having to come to grips with academic English writing at an early age. However, for many students, their first exposure to the discipline is when they have to write an essay as part of their university entrance exams. Naturally, this is not a good time to suddenly be faced with a new form of assessment, and those students that have had practice in academic English writing techniques are at a considerable advantage.

A "statement of purpose" is also an increasingly common requirement for many school and job applications. Furthermore, many of the technical elements of academic English writing are also applicable for letters of application for jobs, and for writing internal and external reports. Thus, whatever route a student intends to take after graduating high school, it makes sense to at least have some grounding in academic English.

Finally, written assignments are one of the most common forms of assessment in many university courses. These most commonly take the form of essays written after the student has conducted individual research and then handed in to the professor, or essays written under exam conditions. Students may also be required to write book reports, literature reviews, film critiques, speeches, dissertations, theses, or complete "gobbets" papers (an exam consisting of a large number of short essay questions). All of these forms of assessment require similar academic English writing skills. Even academic disciplines with quite specific sets of technical writing requirements such as law (legal briefs) and the natural sciences (lab reports) still require basic adherence to the principles of academic English writing.

Then academic English is used at high school, work, university, and at times of transition between these environments. This book, therefore, should be of assistance to many readers.

1.3 The scope of academic English writing

Good academic English writing may be seen as following a set of rules for the construction of a written piece of work. Readers of this book will already be familiar with many of these rules, and they are included here for reference, reinforcement and convenience of use. These include many of the grammatical rules contained in Chapter 2. However, the rules of academic English writing go further than simply requiring adherence to the grammatical rules common to all well-written English. If we consider grammatical rules to be the micro-level building blocks of English writing, academic English writing requires us also to consider how these blocks are fitted together on a macro level. These more structural rules are contained in Chapters 3 and 4.

Academic English writing also requires us to obey certain ethical rules with regard to other people's research and writing. Although some assignments will merely ask for your own impression or point of view, usually you are required to put your own views in perspective. This means that you must at least make reference to the work of others on related issues. In fact, most academic English writing draws on previous research, writings, publications and other materials not only for perspective, but also as sources of evidence and argument. Chapter 5 gives advice on how to track down and evaluate sources of information. When referring to the work of others it is important to give them credit for the direct or indirect contributions they have made to your own work.

Sometimes your reference may be a direct quotation or piece of statistical information taken from somebody else. At other times you may simply be referring to their body of work in more general terms, or paraphrasing something they have previously claimed. Whichever is the case, the rules of academic English require that some form of acknowledgement take place. Chapter 6 advises on the correct (and various) ways to give credit according to different circumstances and traditions. For now, we wish to point out that failure to give proper credit constitutes a breach of the rules of academic English writing, which we call plagiarism, and that this particular breach of the rules is not only frowned upon beyond all other breaches, but can, in fact, have serious academic consequences. Indeed, many universities and individual college professors will fail students for plagiarism regardless of the merits of the rest of their work.

1.4 The scope of this book

There are many books on elements of academic English writing, and also many books aimed at teaching students of English as a foreign language. Indeed, there are dozens of grammar books alone, and the number of reading, writing and conversation books in the TEFL market is constantly growing. However, there are far fewer books focusing on academic English writing for non-native speakers. An academic English writing book written by academics with an inter-disciplinary and international background is a particular rarity. In this book, the authors draw on many years of experience of teaching university courses in the social sciences and humanities, identifying key common failings and addressing them with simple rules, guidelines and models. We thank our students for helping us to identify such needs.

Essentially this book aims to provide a service to non-native English speaking students (although many native speakers could also find useful material within its pages), who are either applying to, or have been accepted into a course in which the teaching medium is English. Top universities in English speaking countries have always attracted a large number of international students. However, recent years have seen a proliferation of university programs taught in English in other countries. This has particularly been the case in countries like Korea, where government initiatives have coincided with the increased cost of studying in English speaking countries and increased security fears.

In keeping with the stated aim of providing a service to the greatest number of students, and in particular to those in greatest need, this book is written in a concise reference manner allowing it to be a compact, valuable and yet affordable tome. We hope that you find it useful, and welcome feedback on how future volumes could further help you in your studies.

1.5 Chapter overview

As this publication is not meant to compete with or replace the many texts and websites that offer comprehensive discussions of proper grammatical usage, Chapter 2 presents only a limited number of grammatical problems that non-native English students often encounter. The purpose of this chapter is not to offer a comprehensive breakdown of these categories, but rather to highlight a few areas where mistakes are frequently made. It is, essentially, a reference chapter which should be consulted when needed, to address particular grammatical problems, or to refresh understanding of particular rules or usages. The twenty issues discussed therein are divided into four categories: parts of speech; punctuation; mechanics; and diction.

The section on speech covers articles (when to use *a*, *an*, and *the*); pronouns (issues with gender, plurality, and ambiguity); verbs (subject/verb agreement and verb tense consistency); adjectives (words that describe or limit nouns or pronouns); adverbs (words that modify a verb, an adjective, or another adverb: advice on avoiding confusion with adjectives); prepositions (verb/preposition agreement and other preposition issues); and conjunctions (review of advanced conjunctions). The section on punctuation covers the use of quotation marks (" " and ' '); commas (,); apostrophes ('); hyphens (-); parentheses (( )); and brackets ([ ]). The section on mechanics covers when to indent paragraphs; when to use capital letters; numerals; and the use of abbreviations. Finally, the section on diction covers common misspellings; commonly confused words; and common academic language usage.

Chapter 3 considers the core structural elements of academic English, sentences and paragraphs. It lays down the rules for the construction of these basic building blocks. The first section considers sentence syntax (basically, this section consists of a list of "don'ts" to be considered when writing sentences). The second section gives constructive advice on what should be done in writing sentences (to a certain extent a list of "do's"). This section covers modifiers; clauses; clause connecters; and active versus passive voice.

The following section (and the rest of the chapter) introduces paragraphs. Simply put, a paragraph is a collection of sentences. More specifically, a paragraph serves to direct the reader to a collection of related ideas contained in a group of sentences. Standard paragraphs usually begin with a statement of the main idea, point or question being addressed. The rest of the paragraph then serves to illustrate the main point, to further develop it, to supply supporting evidence, and or to get down to specifics. Finally, the paragraph should conclude with something of a summary with regard to the collection of ideas that have been addressed. The second half of this chapter addresses the use of topic statements; subject development; summaries; structural links; and paragraph outlines in the construction of paragraphs.

Chapter 4 addresses the most common form of academic writing, the essay. An academic essay is a relatively short piece of work (short enough to be read at a single sitting), that conveys an informed opinion about a single topic. It is not meant to be an all-encompassing treatment of the material. Rather, it is meant to give our opinion about an interesting part of the material. Just as sentences and paragraphs have structure, so too do essays. This chapter covers the construction of the different parts of an academic English essay: introduction; body; and conclusion. It also includes a section on writing balanced essays, and a section on modeling the structure of different forms of academic essays.

Chapter 5 addresses research, and research paper writing. It covers all the stages involved in producing a piece of research work, from choosing a topic and asking questions, through doing the research (finding information) and evaluating sources, to becoming an active reader and an active writer. In terms of the final product, the chapter reviews the steps that a student should take in producing a research paper. These include: brainstorming; free-writing; creating a thesis statement; creating an outline and organizing notes; creating an explanatory draft; revisions, rewriting and preparing a final draft; and the avoidance of plagiarism.

Leading on from the advice on avoiding plagiarism contained in Chapter 5, Chapter 6 addresses acceptable ways to document sources and cite the works of others. As nearly every academic discipline has its own preferred editorial style for formatting, documenting and citing sources, and for listing the works that have been cited, and in many cases there is more than one acceptable format within a discipline, this chapter limits its coverage to the most popular systems used by professors of international studies in their own research and teaching. However, the primary elements of a bibliographic reference are the same for most styles of documentation, although the order in which they are presented may vary. These elements include the name of the author, the title, the place of publication, the publisher's name, the date of publication, and a designation of the location, or page number of a reference. This chapter covers the most common ways in which this information is presented, and also looks at acceptable ways of citing electronic sources.

One caveat is that what is presented herein will likely not address every situation you may encounter. Additionally, in the section on references, many of the citation methods may look similar, however, there are often subtle differences, including the number of spaces required after a period, or the use of single or double spacing. It is advisable, therefore, that as you prepare your document you first consult the style manual, or visit the appropriate official website of each association.

Finally, this book also includes a useful appendix covering the two Romanization systems used by academics to transliterate Korean names and words: the McCune-Reischauer (McC-R) system and the 2000 Revised Romanization of Korean (R) system used by the Korean Government.

Chapter 2 GRAMMAR – Twenty Issues in Academic Writing*

2.1 Introduction

The proper use of grammar is at the very core of good writing, including academic writing. Although the majority of students reading this book will already have a mastery of English, there are certain grammatical situations that can present problems; this is true for non-native and native speakers of English alike. There are many texts and websites that offer comprehensive discussions of proper grammatical usage, some of which are listed at the end of this chapter. These can be referenced for in-depth questions you may have. The aim of this publication, however, is to present only a limited number of grammatical problems that students often encounter.

Essentially, this is a reference chapter. It is not meant to be read straight through in the way that you might read some of the other chapters. Rather, you should consult this chapter when needed, to address particular grammatical problems, or to refresh your understanding of particular rules or usages. It appears at this stage in

* The authors wish to sincerely thank Jacob Reidhead for his diligent and beneficial work in helping prepare this chapter.

the book because a proper understanding of grammar and word usage forms the foundation of all academic writing: it comes before sentences, which come before paragraphs, which come before essays, which come before research papers in terms of size and complexity of construction.

It would, therefore, be perfectly acceptable at this point either to skim forward to the grammatical section that most interests you, or even, to turn to the next chapter, only referring back to this chapter when, in your academic writing, you come up against one of the issues covered herein. However, we do recommend that you, at the very least, make yourself aware of the aspects of grammar that are covered in this chapter. The twenty issues discussed are divided into four categories: parts of speech; punctuation; mechanics; and diction.

2.2 Parts of Speech

Words are the basic building blocks of sentences and ideas. Words can be grouped into various categories known as parts of speech, based on their function within a sentence. Well-known parts of speech include *nouns*, *verbs*, and *adjectives*. The purpose of this chapter is not to offer a comprehensive breakdown of these categories, but rather to highlight a few areas where mistakes are frequently made. This section will focus on five particular areas that frequently cause trouble in academic writing.

1. articles: when to use *a*, *an*, and *the*
2. pronouns: issues with gender, plurality, and ambiguity
3. verbs: subject/verb agreement and verb tense consistency
4. adjectives: order of adjectives in a series
5. adjectives and adverbs: problematic distinctions

6. prepositions: verb/preposition agreement and other preposition issues
7. conjunctions: review of advanced conjunctions

2.2.1 Articles

Deciding when to use *a*, *an*, and *the*, is one of the greatest challenges to non-native speakers and writers of English. *The* is known as the definite article, meaning it is used when a writer refers to a specific instance of a noun. *A* and *an* are known as indefinite articles and refer to nonspecific instances. The decision between *a* and *an* depends on the word following the article. *An* is used if a word begins with a vowel <u>sound</u> (e.g. alarm, hour, egg); if the word begins with a consonant <u>sound</u> (toy, university, European), *a* is used.

Incorrect: President of Korea traveled to China.
Correct: *The* President of Korea traveled to China. (one specific president, for example, the current president)
Correct: *A* President of Korea traveled to China. (not any specific president, but one of many)
Incorrect: I have appointment first weekend of September.
Correct: I have *an* appointment *the* first weekend of September.
Incorrect: We have *a* hour before show starts.
Correct: We have *an* hour before *the* show starts. (hour starts with a vowel sound; this case refers to one specific show)
Correct: We have *an* hour before *a* show starts. (hour still begins with a vowel sound; however one of many shows will start, not one show in particular)

There are two instances in which articles can be omitted: when discussing non-count nouns and when referring to some geographical locations. Non-count nouns include certain foods and drinks (e.g. bread, candy, chicken, fruit, sugar, water, milk), nonfood substances (e.g. air, dirt, paper, rain, wood), abstract nouns (e.g. advice, anger, beauty, employment, information, intelligence, knowledge, love, poverty, truth), and other nouns (e.g. biology and other areas of study, clothing, equipment, homework, violence, work). Non-count nouns cannot generally be categorized into individual units and thus do not require the use of *a, an* or *the*. For instance, a recipe that calls for "one water" would be very confusing, since it is impossible (at least for the average cook) to extract one single water molecule.

Certain geographical names and locations also do not require the use of an article. You can omit *the* when referring to streets, squares, or parks (Iris Avenue, Union Square, Rocky Mountain National Park), cities, states or counties (Boulder, Colorado, Grand County), continents (Asia, South America), bays or single lakes (Salamander Bay, Lake Huron) and single mountains or islands (Mount Fuji, Hawaii). However, you should include *the* when referring to united countries (the United States, the Republic of China), large regions or deserts (the West Coast, the Kalahari), oceans, seas or gulfs (the Pacific, the Persian Gulf), peninsulas (the Korean peninsula), canals or rivers (the Erie Canal, the Nile), mountain ranges (the Alps), and groups of islands (the Solomon Islands).

2.2.2 Pronouns

A *pronoun* is a word that is used in place of a noun, noun phrase or other pronoun without changing the meaning or basic construction of the sentence. Usually the pronoun substitutes a specific noun, known as its *antecedent*. Although the use of pronouns is relatively simple, there are some instances in which pronoun usage can be problematic to academic writers.

2.2.2.1 Gender and Pronouns

Gender specific pronouns must match the gender of their antecedents.

Incorrect: When *you* become pregnant, *you* should cease smoking. (In this case, "you" is referring to women in general, not one specific person with whom one is speaking directly.)

Incorrect: When a woman becomes pregnant, *he* should cease smoking.

Correct: When *a woman* becomes pregnant, *she* should cease smoking.

2.2.2.2 Number and Pronouns

Many indefinite pronouns (e.g. each, any, everyone, someone, nothing) are singular. However, writers are sometimes tempted to refer to these antecedents with plural verbs and pronouns. Whether singular or plural, pronouns and verbs must be consistent and match each other. There are three options for correcting such problems:

- Replace the plural pronoun with *he or she* or *his or her;*
- Make the antecedent plural;
- Rewrite the sentence so that the problem of agreement is resolved.

Incorrect: When *someone* has been drinking, *they* <u>are</u> likely to drive irresponsibly.

Correct 1: When *someone* has been drinking, *he or she* <u>is</u> likely to drive irresponsibly.

Correct 2: When *drivers* have been drinking, *they* are likely to drive irresponsibly.

Correct 3: *A driver who* has been drinking is likely to drive irresponsibly.

Incorrect: A lawyer must study hard if *they* want to pass the bar exam.

Correct 1: A law student must study hard if *he or she* wants to pass the bar exam.

Correct 2: *Law students* must study hard if *they* want to pass the bar exam.

Correct 3: A law student must study hard to pass the bar exam.

2.2.2.3 Well-defined Pronouns

In sentences where compound antecedents are connected by *or, nor*, *either... or,* and *neither... nor*, the pronoun should agree with the nearest antecedent. If one of the antecedents is singular and the other is plural, the plural one should be listed second so as to avoid any awkwardness with the pronoun and verb.

Example: Either Emily or Betty should win first prize for *her* entry in the pie-making contest.

Example: Neither the mouse nor the *rats* found *their* way through the maze.

Ambiguous pronoun reference occurs when the pronoun could refer to two possible antecedents, as in the following examples. One way to avoid this is to ensure that the pronouns and their antecedents are used in close proximity to one another.

Incorrect: When Susie set the vase on the glass-topped table, it broke.

Correct: The vase broke when Susie set it on the glass-topped table.

Another way to avoid pronoun ambiguity is to rewrite the sentence and altogether eliminate the pronoun.

Incorrect: Eun-Young told Su-bin she had won the beauty contest.

Correct: Eun-Young told Su-bin, "You have won the beauty contest."

Other forms of ambiguous reference include references to implied or indefinite antecedents. A pronoun should refer to a specific antecedent, not to a word or idea that is implied, but not referenced directly in the sentence.

Incorrect: After braiding Petunia's hair, Gigi decorated *them* with ribbons.

Correct: After braiding Petunia's hair, Gigi decorated *the braids* with ribbons.

Incorrect: In Shakespeare's Romeo and Juliet, *he* describes the fate of two young lovers.

Correct: In Romeo and Juliet, Shakespeare describes the fate of two young lovers.

2.2.3 Verbs

Verbs are action words that bring life and give power to subjects. A great deal can be said about verbs; however, in this section we focus on two very specific and very common errors in academic writing: subject/verb agreement and verb tense consistency.

2.2.3.1 Subject/Verb Agreement

Matching the appropriate verb form with its corresponding subject is a challenge to both native and foreign writers of English. While sundry rules and exceptions can complicate the problem, the vast majority of mistakes can be avoided by ensuring that every verb in every sentence agrees with its corresponding subject in both person and number. The sentences below provide examples of subject/verb conflict:

Incorrect: *The play*, now showing every weekend, *take* a long time to prepare.

Correct: *The play*, now showing every weekend, *took* a long time to prepare.

Incorrect: *Each of you receive* a letter of congratulation for your participation.

Correct: *Each of you receives* a letter of congratulation for your participation.

2.2.3.2 Verb Conjugation

Verb tenses must be consistent so long as the tense (past, present) of the sentence is constant. In some languages, given a list of verbs in a sentence, only the final verb is conjugated for tense. In English, however, so long as tense is constant throughout the sentence, every verb must be properly conjugated. Consider the following examples:

Incorrect: Yesterday I **go** to the store, **buy** salami, and **returned** home.

Incorrect: Yesterday I **went** to the store, **buy** salami, and **return** home.

Correct: Yesterday I **went** to the store, **bought** salami, and **returned** home.

Each event in the list occurred in the past and must be conjugated for past tense. At the same time, tense should not to be confused with aspect (perfect and progressive) nor modal auxiliaries (*may*, *might*, *could*, *should*, *would*, *will*, etc.). Unlike tenses, these words only appear before the first verb in a list, but they apply to all. Compare the examples below with those above:

> Tomorrow I ***shall*** **go** to the store, **buy** salami, and **return** home.
> **(*modal auxiliary* + present tense)**

> Many times before, I ***had*** **gone** to the store, **bought** salami, and **returned** home.
> **(past perfect → *perfect aspect* + past tense)**

Notice in both of the examples above, the modal auxiliary, *shall*, and the indicator of perfect aspect, *had*, appear only once in each sentence respectively, immediately before the first verb in each list. Furthermore, notice, as with the original examples, that tense is consistent throughout both sentences, present in the first (*go*, *buy*, *return*) and past in the second (*gone*, *bought*, *returned*). The list of rules governing verb conjugation is far more extensive than we have space to address here. Nonetheless, adherence to the elementary principles of verb conjugation addressed above resolves a significant ratio of mistakes found in academic writing.

2.2.4 Adjective Order in a Series

An adjective is a word that describes or limits a noun or pronoun. In other words, an adjective places a restriction on the noun. For instance, the word *purple* in the phrase "the purple turtle" not only describes the turtle, it also limits the focus onto a particular turtle –

specifically, the purple one. Often, an adjective answers one or more of the following questions:

How many?
What kind of?
Which?

Adjectives are often found in a series in English (e.g. Clifford, the *big*, *red* dog), but as a non-native speaker (and even for many native speakers) it is difficult to understand why the adjectives should fall in a particular order, and how to determine the correct order. For instance, one might say "I ate a big, round, juicy blueberry," but to say "I ate a round, juicy, big blueberry" would be incorrect. The following guidelines can be used to help determine in what order adjectives should fall. Although there are always exceptions to the rule, this chart can serve as a standard.

1. **Determiners:** articles and other limiters
2. **Observations:** post-determiners and limiting adjectives (e.g., a real hero, a perfect idiot) and adjectives subject to subjective measure (e.g., beautiful, interesting)
3. **Sizes and Shapes:** adjectives subject to objective measure (e.g., wealthy, large, round)
4. **Age:** adjectives denoting age (e.g., young, old, new, ancient)
5. **Colors:** adjectives denoting color (e.g., red, black, pale)
6. **Origins:** adjectives denoting source of noun (e.g., French, American, Canadian)
7. **Materials:** adjectives denoting what something is made of (e.g., woolen, metallic, wooden)
8. **Qualifiers:** final limiter, often regarded as part of the noun (e.g., rocking chair, hunting cabin, passenger car, book cover)

In the following examples, notice the order of adjectives, which are arranged according to categories listed above:

a gorgeous new Italian sports car
an expensive antique ruby ring
six aromatic long-stemmed red roses
those round paper hat boxes
several strong young Korean soccer players

2.2.5 Confusable Adjectives and Adverbs

In general the distinction between adjectives and adverbs is quite clear, as the former describe or limit a noun or pronoun, and the latter modify a verb, an adjective, or another adverb. Depending on the construction of the sentence, an adverb can also modify a preposition, a conjunction, a noun, or a pronoun. There are a few instances, however, in which adjectives and adverbs can be confused, as in the following cases:

2.2.5.1 fewer vs. less: fewer refers to items that can be counted, whereas less refers to general amounts.

Fewer people are living in the countryside these days.
There was *less* cream filling in my Oreos than I had hoped.

2.2.5.2 good vs. well: good is an adjective, whereas *well* is an adverb. Therefore, when modifying a verb, use the adverb *well.* However, when using a linking verb or a verb that has to do with the five human senses, use an adjective. Many academic writers will also use the adverb *well* when writing or speaking about one's health, as in the fourth sentence below:

He looks good in that sweater. (adjective)
She speaks Korean well. (adverb)
Babies smell so good after a bath. (linking verb, smell = adjective)
I am feeling well, thank you. (regarding health = adverb)

The differences between good and well will be addressed again in Section 19 (Commonly Confused Words).

2.2.5.3 bad vs. badly: the same rule applies for bad/badly as good/well. *Bad* is an adjective, whereas *badly* in an adverb.

She felt *bad* that she was late and missed the performance.
His leg hurt *badly* after he slid into home plate.

2.2.5.4 Do not use *more* with a comparative adjective formed with *-er* (e.g. do not write that something is *more darker*).

2.2.5.5 Do not use *most* with a superlative adjective formed with *–est* (e.g. do not write that something is *most ugliest.*)

2.2.6 Prepositions

While conjunctions connect clauses, prepositions connect a single object, known as the object of the preposition, to another sentence element. Common examples of simple prepositions include *in*, *under*, *around*, and *above*. A prepositional phrase consists of the preposition, the object of the preposition, and any modifiers, as in the phrases "to the grocery store," "over the rainbow," and "for the past twenty years." First, this section addresses the major issue of verb/preposition agreement. Second, it introduces the two advanced categories of prepositions, participial and phrasal, which, when used effectively, enhance the level and sophistication of academic writing.

2.2.6.1 Verb/Preposition Agreement

Matching verbs with the appropriate preposition can be difficult, especially considering that many verb/preposition pairs are colloquial rather than intuitive. A list of commonly confused verb/preposition pairs is provided below:

accompanied by (with a person)**:** The king was accompanied by his lovely queen.

according to (in accordance with)**:** You will be punished according to the law.

agree on (a matter)**:** My mom and dad fight continually. They can't agree on anything.

agree to (a proposal)**:** The school board agrees with your proposal to fund a chess club.

agree with (a person)**:** I agree with your point that pigeon tastes like chicken.

angry at, about (a situation)**:** We were all angry about the way you were treated.

angry with (a person)**:** Is Simon still angry with me for leaving his party early?

beside (by the side of)**:** The old mill sat beside the river, a specter of times past.

besides (in addition to)**:** Besides cake, we also serve pie and ice cream.

compare to (to liken)**:** We compared the Gothic library to an ancient monolith of yore.

compare with (to examine for similarities)**:** If we compare these blood splatter patterns with those at the crime scene, we notice some remarkable similarities.

concentrate on, upon (to focus)**:** Ladies and gentlemen, please concentrate your attention on the man floating in the middle of the room.

contrast (n) **between:** The contrast between their personalities is like night and day.

contrast (v) **to:** Contrast your bad feelings for him with your good feelings for me.

correspond to (things)**:** The *han* in Korean society corresponds to the sorrow experienced by the Jewish people.

correspond with (a person)**:** Our grandmother corresponds with us regularly via email.

foreign to: Having grown up in the desert, the humidity in Tokyo is foreign to me.

graduate (v) **from:** When will you graduate from high school?

graduate (n) **of:** My cousin is a graduate of Ewha Womans University.

independent of: Throughout the early twentieth century, many Koreans struggled to be independent of Japanese occupation.

join in (participate)**:** We are baking pies. Please join in and make some with us.

join to (connect)**:** Join this cable to the back of your computer and turn it on.

join with (associate)**:** In America, a person may join with a political party at the age of eighteen.

plan to (followed by a verb): This summer our colleagues plan to vacation near the East Sea.

proficient in: Taekwondo masters are often proficient in several forms of martial arts.

reason (v) **about** (an issue)**:** Algebraists must be able to reason about abstract concepts in multiple dimensions.

reason (n) **for** (an action)**:** The reason for the L.A. riot was rooted in the Rodney King beating.

reason (v) **with** (a person)**:** Teenagers are typically difficult to reason with.

sensitive to: Claustrophobic patients are sensitive to small and cramped spaces.

separate from: I do not recommend married couples separate from one another longer than necessary.

speak to (communicate a fact)**:** Will any board members speak to the issue of cleaning out the swimming pool?

speak with (converse)**:** Joanie, may I speak with you for a moment?

talk to (lecture)**:** I prefer a professor that opens discussion rather than just talks to the class.

talk with (converse)**:** My parents would like to talk with us this evening.

2.2.6.2 Participial Prepositions

Participial prepositions are verbs written in the participial form (+ing) and used as prepositions. Some participial prepositions include:

assuming	following
beginning	including
considering	involving
excluding	regarding

Consider the following examples:

Example: My family reunion, *involving* relatives from four generations back, began yesterday.

Example: All students, *excluding* those in detention, will attend the assembly.

Example: Your willingness to volunteer, *considering* the danger of the situation, was quite noble and brave.

2.2.6.3 Phrasal Prepositions

A phrasal preposition is a phrase comprised of a string of words that function as a single preposition. Such phrases are generally accepted colloquially and are rarely modified. Some phrasal prepositions include:

by way of	in case of
in place of	on behalf of
in spite of	in addition to

Consider the following examples:

Example: May I have the salmon in place of the steak?
Example: Use the stairs in the case of an emergency.
Example: On behalf of the council, I present you with this honorary gift towel.

2.2.7 Conjunctions

Conjunctions connect and establish relationships between single words, groups of words, and independent clauses. The simplest conjunctions, *and*, *but*, and *or* are known as coordinating conjunctions and are relatively simple to use; however, in more sophisticated composition, selecting and implementing the appropriate conjunction can be challenging. Nevertheless, careful and creative use of conjunctions greatly improves the quality of academic writing. This section will review two advanced families of conjunctions: adverbial conjunctions and correlative conjunctions.

2.2.7.1 Adverbial Conjunctions

Adverbial conjunctions are used to connect two independent clauses. An independent clause is an expression that can stand alone as a complete sentence. Accordingly, adverbial conjunctions can be used either mid-sentence, or at the beginning of a new sentence. Below is a list of common adverbial conjunctions:

Consequently	Nevertheless
Furthermore	Then
However	Therefore
Moreover	Thus

We begin with two related, but independent clauses:

Example 1: I recently survived being struck by lightning. I no longer golf in the rain.
Example 2: We have no money. We must eat.

Among the many options, we may choose to employ the conjunctions *consequently* and *nevertheless*, respectively. When used mid-sentence, adverbial conjunctions are preceded by a semicolon and followed by a comma.

Example 1: I recently survived being struck by lightning; *consequently*, I no longer golf in the rain.
Example 2: We have no money; *nevertheless*, we must eat.

When used at the beginning of a sentence, adverbial conjunctions are always followed by a comma.

Example 1: I recently survived being struck by lightning. *Consequently*, I no longer golf in the rain.

Example 2: We have no money. *Nevertheless*, we must eat.

2.2.7.2 Correlative Conjunctions

Correlative conjunctions function in the same way as other conjunctions, with the exception that they work in pairs. Correlative conjunctions include the following:

either…or
neither…nor
whether…or
both…and
not only…but also

Consider the examples below:

It will *either* rain *or* snow tomorrow.
Whether we go to the library *or* eat lunch first, we need to leave soon.

When making negative comparisons, use *nor* in place of or.

Incorrect: *Neither* John ***or*** Julie came to the party.
Correct: *Neither* John ***nor*** Julie came to the party.

When using correlative conjunctions, the verb should agree with the nearest noun. If one part of the subject is singular and the other is plural, put the plural one last to avoid confusion (see also Section 3b). Consider the following examples:

Neither Harold *nor* Maude **eats** cake.
Neither the dog *nor* the cat **was** able to catch the mouse.
Neither the dog *nor* our three cats **were** able to catch the mouse.

2.3 Punctuation

Punctuation is a set of tools offered a writer to enhance expression and add clarity to writing. In this section, we address five common trouble spots:

8. quotation marks (“ ” and ‘ ’)
9. commas (,)
10. apostrophes (’)
11. hyphens (-)
12. parentheses (( ))
13. brackets ([ ])

2.3.1 Quotation Marks

Quotation marks are primarily used for identifying quotations taken word for word from an outside source. A comprehensive reference on citations, quotations, and referencing can be found in Chapter 6 of this publication. Here we address a few specific errors regarding the use of quotation marks.

2.3.1.1 First, some writers tend to place quotations within brackets (< >) rather than quotation marks (“ ”). This method is incorrect; quotations should always be identified by quotation marks (“ ” or ‘ ’). Furthermore, the use of single quotation marks (‘ ’) should be restricted to a quotation inside of a quotation; double quotation marks should be used in all other cases. Consider the examples below:

Incorrect: My favorite movie is <Black Beauty,> said Joe.
Correct: My favorite movie is “Black Beauty,” said Joe.
Incorrect: ‘What,’ asked Maria, ‘is the nature of your visit?’
Correct: “What,” asked Maria, “is the nature of your visit?”
Incorrect: Joe stated, “Maria asked me, why did you come here?”
Correct: Joe stated, “Maria asked me, ‘Why did you come here?’”

2.3.1.2 Another challenging aspect of quotation marks relates to whether periods, commas, question marks and exclamation marks fall inside or outside of the quotation marks at the end of a quote. Periods and commas following a quote are always included within the quote. Exclamation marks and question marks are included if the nature of the quote itself is exclamatory or interrogative. If the exclamatory or interrogative quality arises from a part of the sentence other than the quote, these marks are placed outside the quotation marks. The examples below should help clarify:

Example: Does the author honestly believe “to be or not to be, that is the question”?
Example: The cover of the video case said, “beautiful, stunning, a masterpiece.”

2.3.1.3 Additional uses of quotations include enclosing slang and coined, technical, or ironic expressions.

Example: Yet another “groovy” idea from the “slickster.”
Example: I’m dealing the cards. Are you “in”?
Example: You can play, but don’t shoot the ball. You “brick”

more than a mason.

Example: I love the "invisible hand," but I know it is not perfect.

2.3.2 Commas

The comma is the most common form of internal punctuation. Confusion about where or where not to used commas often results in incorrect usage. The following rules and accompanying examples are by no means comprehensive, but will hopefully elucidate the primary uses and abuses of the comma.

2.3.2.1 The comma functions to separate words, phrases, and clauses written in a series. A comma *is* placed before the conjunction separating the last two items in the list.

Example: This summer I visited Kyôngju, Boryông, and the Korean War Museum.

Example: Paul swept the floor, I washed the dishes, and then we both watched a movie.

Example: We buy groceries at E-Mart, in the market downtown, and at the corner mart.

2.3.2.2 Parenthetical expressions, adjective clauses, participial phrases, and introductory adverb clauses are all set off by commas.

Example: On the other hand, perhaps we should go to the funeral.

Example: Our old principal, who retired last year, attended the football game.

Example: The friends, moved by their reunion, promised to keep in touch regularly.

Example: As long as it is raining, we will not go out to play football.

2.3.2.3 Commas should also be used to separate individual elements of dates and addresses, as well as after numbers greater than three digits. In large numbers, every three digits are grouped using a comma from right to left.

Example: I was born April 30, 1975, at 24 Connery Lane, Edinburgh, Scotland.
Example: 1,024
Example: 40,284,918

2.3.3 Apostrophes

Apostrophes are used to form possessives (Joe's Crab Shack) and contractions (e.g. can't, they're, I'm). This section will review the rules for making possessives of singular and plural nouns.

2.3.3.1 To make singular nouns possessive, add an apostrophe and an *s*.

Examples:
Dr. Smellgood's deodorant
Gus's motorcycle
the mailman's bag
Yang-hyuk's homework
mattress's tag
Mrs. Robinson's swimming pool

2.3.3.2 In the case of plural nouns, write the noun; if the form ends in an *s*, simply add an apostrophe; if not, add an apostrophe and then an *s*.

Examples:
men's coats
children's toys
fish's tail
cats' eyes
all the Jones' homes

2.3.4 Hyphens

The hyphen is used to connect particles and words to other words. This section provides a few fundamental guidelines for correct hyphen use.

2.3.4.1 Hyphens can link a string of words that function as a single adjective modifier:

Examples:
grand-slam breakfast
up-to-date records
50-yard line
over-the-top performance
under-the-table transaction

2.3.4.2 Hyphens are used when writing out numbers twenty-one through ninety-nine.

2.3.4.3 Hyphens are used to attach a prefix to a proper noun:

Examples:
anti-Japanese
pro-Cuban
un-American
pre-20th Century
post-Modernism

2.3.4.4 When connecting a prefix to a root word, hyphens are used if the first letter of the root word and the last letter of the prefix are the same, or if the root word begins with *w*:

Examples:
co-organize
re-energize
pre-elementary
co-worker
preconditioning
semi-included
deconstruct
post-war

2.3.4.5 Dividing a word at the end of a line can also be done using hyphens, and must follow the guidelines below:

- **Do** divide words between pronounceable parts, namely syllables.
  Incorrect: subst- itute
  Corrrect: sub- stitute (or) substi- tute
  Incorrect: fore- ver
  Correct: for- ever

- **Do** divide words having prefixes or suffixes between the prefix or suffix and root word:
  Example: un- forgettable; ex- Marine
- **Do** divide words containing double consonants by the consonant:
  Examples: collision col- lision; parrot par- rot
- **Do not** divide proper names, titles, initials, or first and last names.
- **Do not** divide words so that a single letter stands alone:
  Incorrect: a- lone; e- veryone

2.3.5 Parentheses

Parentheses may be used to enclose (1) parenthetical phrases that are loosely connected with to the sentence, (2) references, directions, and additional explanations, (3) figures repeated to ensure accuracy, and (4) figures or letters used to mark divisions or counted lists (as in this sentence). Consider the examples below:

Example (parenthetical phrase): I am not certain (I should be more knowledgeable on the subject) that Columbus was in fact right handed.

Example (parenthetical phrase): Critics of Eminem (many of whom have not even listened to his music) say his popularity stems from his being white rather than his talent.

Example (references): We will meet in front of the Hyundae Department Store (Apgujeong Station, exit 6) at seven o'clock.

Example (references): The section on citations (see Chapter 7) ought to answer any questions you have about constructing a bibliography.

Example (figures): I only spent fifty pounds (£50) on this couch.

2.3.6 Brackets

Where parentheses are used to append content-related ideas, brackets are used to edit technical discrepancies or changes.

2.3.6.1 Brackets can enclose missing or vague information within a quotation:

Example: "We must fight it [hunger] until it no longer threatens our country, our families, and especially our children."

2.3.6.2 Brackets can be used to grammatically alter words in a quotation so that it maybe incorporated into another sentence.

Example:
(original quote) "I think; therefore, I am." (Rene Descartes)
(altered) According to Descartes, "[We] think; therefore, [we are]."

2.3.6.3 Brackets can be used to correct mistakes made in another text.

Example: "Allied Forces fought the Russians [Germans] in the Battle of the Bulge."

2.4 Mechanics

Mechanics covers the more technical, nuts and bolts aspects of writing such as the physical shape and form of words, sentences, and paragraphs. As with the earlier sections, this sections is by no means comprehensive; nonetheless, hopefully the topics below will be instrumental in avoiding common and easily avoidable errors:

14. indenting paragraphs
15. capital letters
16. numerals
17. abbreviations

2.4.1 Indenting Paragraphs

When writing academically, we build upward from words, to sentences, and on to paragraphs. Just as a sentence begins with a capital letter and ends with a punctuation mark, paragraphs begin with an indentation of several spaces. We often press the *Tab* button once to perform this more conveniently. Only the first line of a paragraph needs indenting; all other lines should begin flush with the left margin. Unless specified otherwise by the journal or conference to which the paper is being submitted, we recommend this format for all forms of academic writing. Only in a few special cases, such as with block quotations (see Chapter 6) will you be required to indent an entire paragraph.

2.4.2 Capital Letters

Capitalizing letters is done to distinguish certain words from the rest of the sentence. A comprehensive list of rules of what to capitalize is rather lengthy. Here we identify the most common instances.

2.4.2.1 The first word of any sentence should always be capitalized.

2.4.2.2 The first word of any direct quotation only when the beginning of the sentence is included:

Examples:
Elliot shuddered, "It's revolting!"
Clark posits the best way to run a race is, "with your eyes open."
Golfers' Travails begins, "Long ago on the links far, far away…"

2.4.2.3 The first word and any noun in the salutation of a letter must be capitalized.

Example: Dear Family and Friends,

2.4.2.4 Only the first word of a complimentary close should be capitalized.

Example: Yours truly,

2.4.2.5 Initials, the names of people, titles (and abbreviations of titles) that proceed or follow proper names, and the titles and abbreviations of academic degrees and high government offices should all be capitalized.

Examples:
Mr. John Williams, Jr.
Lady Jane Eyre, Ph.D.
Dr. Lloyd Bishop, Sr.
Masters of Science degree
Secretary of Defense

2.4.2.6 Geographical names, the names of firms, institutions, organizations, buildings, brand names, historical events and periods, holidays, government bodies, races, religions, nationalities, the names of languages, and the abbreviations of proper nouns are also all capitalized.

Examples:

Pyongyang, DPRK	Constitution Day
Microsoft	U.S. House of Representatives
Ewha Womans University	African
Boy Scouts of America	Christian
Trump Towers	WWII
Dark Ages	LAPD

2.4.3 Numerals

Deciding when to spell out numerals or simply write them as numbers depends on the few rules below:

2.4.3.1 For the numerals one to ninety-nine, several conventions exist. Each convention is equal; once one has been selected, however, it is important to be consistent.

- One convention is to write out the numbers one to ninety-nine and represent the rest with numerical symbols.
- Another convention is to write out only the numbers one through twenty.
- A third convention is to write out only one through ten.

2.4.3.2 When writing lists that contain numbers, consistency is most important; either write all the numbers out or represent them as numerical symbols.

Incorrect: I purchased 20 golf clubs, 100 golf balls, and two bags.

Correct: Our high school boasted 600 freshmen, 545 sophomores, 531 juniors, and 495 seniors.

2.4.3.3 It is best to represent numerals as numerical symbols when a sentence or paragraph contains a large list of numbers, and where writing them out would create unsightly text.

Incorrect: The heights of Brownsville High's starting basketball team were six foot four inches, six foot two inches, six foot one inch, six foot four inches, and six foot six inches.

Correct: The heights of Brownsville High's starting basketball team were 6'4", 6'2", 6'1", 6'4", and 6'6".

2.4.3.4 A sentence should never begin with a symbolic number. As a result, there may be times when it is more convenient to place the number later in the sentence.

Incorrect: 1,024 cherry trees dot the banks of the Sweetness River.

Correct: One thousand twenty-four cherry trees dot the banks of the Sweetness River.

Incorrect: One million five hundred thirty-two thousand nine hundred seventy-three people live in the city of Halloway.

Correct: The population of the city of Halloway is 1,532,973.

2.4.3.5 In the following instances, numbers should be represented symbolically even if they normally would be written out:

- Percents and decimals
- Physical quantities (distances, masses, speeds, etc.)
- Sums of money
- Dates

2.4.3.6 The numerical designations of centuries (twenty-first century, seventeenth century) are written out in letters.

2.4.4 Abbreviations

In casual writing situations (e.g. emails to friends and short text messages) there is a tendency to use abbreviations that are not generally acceptable in academic writing. For instance, writing the contracted version of Christmas as Xmas, or using Fri. in place of Friday. Some writers even include *chat-room-like* lingo in their academic writing (see you → cu, laugh out loud → lol, because → cuz). While English does allow certain words, titles, or names to be abbreviated, indiscriminate shortcuts, particularly in academic writing, is strongly discouraged.

The following is a list of categories of abbreviations that contain periods:

- Professional titles: Dr., Ph.D., M.A., J.D., R.N.
- A.M., P.M., A.D., B.C., P.S.
- Latin notation: i.e., e.g., etc., sic.

- First and middle names of people: T.S. Eliot, George H.W. Bush

The following categories are abbreviated and do not contain periods:

- Radio or television call letters: SBS, KBS
- Organizations and government agencies: NKCTPA, FBI, CIA, BSA, NYPD

Again, we discourage the unconventional application of creative abbreviations, particularly within academic writing.

2.5 Diction

The remaining three topics pertain to the topics of diction, or word choice. Specifically, this section provides three lists of words that are either frequently misspelled, mistaken for another word of similar pronunciation or spelling, or translated incorrectly or in a confusing way. These lists are in no way comprehensive. Thus, we encourage you, the writer, to personalize these lists by adding instances of words as you recognize them in your own writing or the writing of others that you commonly mistake or confuse.

18. common misspellings
19. commonly confused pairs
20. common academic language usage

2.5.1 Common Misspellings

The following words are commonly misspelled by both native and non-native writers of English alike:

accessible
accommodate
achieve
acquire
affect
all right
a lot (not alot)
analyze
beginning
believable
business
challenge
changeable
committee
comparative
conceivable
connoisseur
conscience
conscious
convenient
deceive
definitely
dependent
description
desirable
disappear
effect
especially
experience
explanation
formerly
forty
generally
independent
irrelevant
judgment
knowledge
minimum
noticeable
occasion
occasionally
occurred
occurrence
opinion
particular
peaceable
performance
possesses
preceding
preferred
privilege
probably
pronunciation
quantity
receive
receiving
referring
relieve
rhyme
rhythm
schedule
separate
severely
similar
sincerely
specifically
studying
succeed
therefore
too
unconscious
unnecessary
usually
whether
woman
women

2.5.2 Commonly Confused Words

The following pairs of words are commonly confused either because they sound similar, or the writer is not sure which of the two is appropriate in what situations:

a, an: Use *a* before words beginning with a consonant sound and *an* before words beginning with a vowel sound.

accept, except: *Accept* means *to receive. Except* means *to exclude.*

Example: We accept your application for the 2005 school year.

Example: We have all this dress in every color except red.

advice, advise: *Advice* is a noun and refers to a suggestion of how to act. *Advise* is the act of suggesting a course of action.

Example: Friends and family are endless source of advice when it comes to getting married.

Example: Toby's department counselor advised him to take another math class.

affect, effect: *Affect* is a verb meaning "to influence or have some impact on." *Effect* is both a noun and a verb. Effect as a noun means "result" and as a verb means "to bring to pass."

Example: What will be the effect of this year's drought on Ohio's wheat crop?

Example: How will this year's drought affect Ohio's wheat crop?

Example: This policy change ought to effect a decrease in drunken driving.

complement, compliment: *Complement* means "that which

completes or accents, a full or total number"; to *compliment* is to flatter or make a flattering statement.

Example: The green curtains complement the cream wallpaper.

Example: Julie, I would like to compliment you on your recent piano recital.

conscience, conscious: *Conscious* means "being awake, alert"; *conscience* refers to a person's inner moral feelings about right and wrong.

Example: At first I did not consciously recognize my elementary school teacher, but I knew I had seen her somewhere before.

Example: My conscience urged me to return the extra change I had been given.

farther, further: *Farther* denotes distance. *Further* expresses the meaning of "more, in addition, to a greater degree."

Example: My legs are so tired that I cannot walk any farther.

Example: If we push the project deadline back any further, we'll never finish.

first, firstly (second, secondly): Both are accepted words in the English language. When listing the steps in a process, first, second, third, and so on are preferable to firstly, secondly, etc.

Example: First, we must consider the cultural context in which the author lived. Second, we should take into account her personal life experiences.

good, well: *Good* is a noun or an adjective and should not be used as an adverb. *Well* functions both as an adjective and an adverb.

Example: He looks good in black.

Example: She looks well today. (meaning, she looks healthy today.)

Incorrect Example: He writes good. (Here, good acts incorrectly as an adverb.)

Example: He writes good poetry. (Here, good is correctly used as an adjective to describe poetry.)

Example: He writes well. (Here, well is used correctly as an adverb describing how he writes.)

I, me: *I* and *me* are both first person pronouns. I is used as subject; me is used as an object.

Example: *I* like Bob and Bob likes *me*.

loose, lose: *Loose*, as a verb, means "to set free" and as an adjective means "free, not fastened"; *lose* is a verb that means "to cease having."

Example: Loose your shoe strings and take off your shoes.

Example: Where did you lose your wallet?

passed, past: *Passed* means "exceeded, gained the lead" or "caused someone to receive something." *Past* means "(in) a bygone time."

Example: The final exam was so difficult that no one passed.

Example: In the past, one could buy a candy bar for a nickel.

than, then: *Than* is a conjunction used in comparisons; *then* is an adverb used to refer to a period or moment of time.

Example: She is faster than he.

Example: First, the sun comes up and dries up all the rain; then the teensy, weensy spider climbs up the spout again.

that, which: *That* and *which* are not to be used interchangeably. That should only be used to introduce a restrictive clause and which for a nonrestrictive clause.

Example: The chili that I cooked was enjoyed by all. (Here, the use of the word *that* restricts the reference of chili to the one that the writer cooked.)

Example: The chili which I cooked was enjoyed by all. (Here, only one dish of chili is being referenced. *Which* does not restrict the reference and simply describes the chili.)

there, their, they're: *There* is an adverb specifying place or an expletive. *Their* is a possessive pronoun, and *they're* is a contraction of they are.

Example: There is a painting by my younger sister.

Example: Master Lao lives over there.

Example: We tripped over their backpacks coming in.

Example: Look at our children: They're the hope of the future.

to, too, two: *To* is a preposition; *too* is an adverb; *two* is a number.

Example: Let's go to the store.

Example: Last night my colleague consumed too much alcohol.

Example: Two birds flew over the cuckoo's nest.

who, whom: *Who* is used for subjects and subject complements. *Whom* is used for objects.

Example: Who would like to attend the opera this evening?

Example: Whom did you have in mind?

Example: We honor those who fought the good fight.

Example: With whom did you study?

2.5.3 Common Academic Languages Usage

Translating thoughts from one language into another can be very challenging, particularly for advanced topics and writing styles. Much academic writing, however, is formulaic, meaning that certain forms and structures tend to be repeated from paper to paper. This section offers a short list of grammatical forms widely used in academic writing. We encourage serious writers to personalize the list, adding expressions frequently found in their own writing. A conscious effort to identify patterns in one's own writing will likely save time in the future and help the writer to improve his or her style. The patterns below are organized in the order they might appear in an academic thesis.

Title page

- This research was supported in part by…
- Correspondence should be addressed to…

Abstract

- This paper will focus on…
- In this paper, (I) we show that…
- Recent studies (recent research) has shown that…
- In recent years…

Outline

- The rest of this paper is organized as follows…
- Section two discusses previous research and background information…
- In chapter three we analyze…
- Chapter four contains our results…

- We conclude in chapter five with a final discussion and suggestions for future work.

Citing sources

- According to the sources cited in…
- According to Bates (1964)…
- Standish (2003) claims that…
- Using data taken from Buford (1984, 32) we…

Drawing Conclusions

- Interestingly enough…
- They explain that…
- We assert that…
- Our data suggests that…
- From (the results in)... it is apparent that…
- These results lead us to conclude that…
- This can be interpreted to mean…
- Based on…, we conclude that…
- Consistent with…, we show that…
- The following is a summary of our results.

2.6 Conclusion

As has been stressed throughout this chapter, the issues presented here represent only a small fraction of grammatical rules and problems that can exist in academic writing. The purpose of the chapter is to offer a brief resource for non-native writers. Specifically, the issues covered in this chapter represent problems that are often faced by student writers – even those who are proficient speakers of

English – as they prepare academic essays and research papers. If a student will master the twenty issues presented in this chapter, her English writing skills will improve, enabling her to investigate further issues on her own.

References

Hacker, Diana. 1998. *The Bedford Handbook*, 5th ed. Boston, MA: Bedford Books.

Loberger, Gordon and Kate Shoup Welsh. 2002. *Webster's New World English Grammar Handbook.* Indianapolis, IN: Wiley Publishing, Inc.

Other Grammar References, Guides, and Useful Websites

Capital Community College Foundation. 2004. *The Guide to Grammar and Writing*. Hartford, CT. <http://webster.commnet.edu/grammar/index.htm>.

Clear English. 2003. *Grammar.* <http://www.clearenglish.net/grammar.htm>.

Hurford, James R. 1994. *Grammar: A Student's Guide*. Cambridge, England: University of Cambridge Press.

Purdue University Online Writing Lab. 2005. *Grammar, Punctuation, and Spelling.*
<http://owl.english.purdue.edu/handouts/grammar/>.

Straus, Jane. 2005. *The Blue Book of Grammar and Punctuation.* Mill Valley, CA. <http://www.grammarbook.com/grammar/cnt_gram.asp>.

Strunk, William, Jr. [1979] 2000. *The Elements of Style*, 4th ed.

Needham Heights, MA: Allyn and Bacon.

Strunk, William, Jr. n.d. *The Elements of Style*. <http://www.bartleby.com/141/>.

Wardhaugh, Ronald. 1995. *Understanding English Grammar: A Linguistic Approach*. Cambridge, MA: Blackwell Publishers.

Chapter 3 Sentences and Paragraphs

3.1 Introduction

In this chapter we will consider the core structural elements of academic English; sentences and paragraphs. For many of the readers of this book, you may feel that such elementary concepts are beneath the level of English competence you have thus far achieved. However, in the authors' wide and varied experience, it is often the construction and placement of these very building blocks that cause problems for our students, and undermine the credentials of what would otherwise have been a fine piece of academic writing.

In general, much of our sentence and paragraph structure occurs unconsciously. Earlier reading and writing may have given us a "feel" for the way words should fit together to express what we want to say. Sometimes, to get thoughts straight in their heads, human beings will mentally construct sentences, or even paragraphs. So a degree of what we will cover in this chapter may seem intuitive. Yet what may intuitively seem right, may also, on occasion, be wrong in terms of academic English writing.

Academic writing requires a much more precise formulation of sentences than we are generally used to carrying out in conversation, informal writing, e-mails or text-messaging. We may also, through a variety of media and practices have been exposed to poor sentence and paragraph structure. What makes perfect sense in one context may not readily be transferable to another context. That is why, even if we do not use them on a day to day basis, it is important to know the rules of formal writing. In learning the rules of sentence and paragraph, we can convey what we mean not only more clearly, but also more convincingly, due to the preciseness of the wording.

3.2 Sentence Syntax

The parts of speech covered in Chapter 2 are the basic building blocks of sentences. Syntax refers to the principles that govern how these blocks are arranged to form sentences. As with parts of speech, a comprehensive treatment of sentence syntax would fill hundreds of pages. Rather than exhaust the countless intricacies of constructing proper sentences, this section will address seven areas where mistakes are frequently made. Firm understanding and application of even these few fundamentals lay a solid foundation for improving one's academic writing. Basically, this section consists of a list of "don'ts" to be considered when writing sentences. The following section (3.3) gives constructive advice on what should be done in writing sentences: a list of "do's" to a certain extent.

1. avoid sentence fragments
2. avoid run-on sentences
3. avoid beginning sentences with *but*, *and*, *also*, and *so*
4. adjectives and adjective clauses
5. avoid double negatives
6. avoid dangling participles
7. avoid postponed prepositions

3.2.1 Avoid Sentence Fragments

Phrases and dependent clauses describe, clarify, and add color to sentences; however, these elements of sentence structure are not complete sentences themselves. Often the fragment describes some element in an earlier sentence. In this case, it may be easiest to join the fragment with that sentence, as in the examples below:

Incorrect: "Drink your milk. And your orange juice."
Correct: "Drink your milk, and your orange juice."
Incorrect: We tracked him for days. Over the mountains, across the tundra.
Correct: We tracked him for days, over the mountains, across the tundra.

Sentence fragments can also be corrected to form a new, complete sentence. In order to become complete sentences, phrases and dependent clauses require more information in the form of an independent clause. Consider the examples below:

Incorrect: If you do rock climb this weekend.
Correct: If you do rock climb this weekend, I want to go with you.
Incorrect: At the office building on Jefferson and Grand.
Correct: Jeffrey works at the office building on Jefferson and Grand.

3.2.2 Avoid Run-on Sentences

While sentence fragments lack an independent clause, run-on sentences typically contain too many. Several independent clauses joined together in one sentence can create long and awkward run-on sentences. Sometimes, adding the appropriate punctuation within the sentence can solve the problem. At other times, simply dividing the run-on sentence into two or more separate sentences is best. The examples below demonstrate how to identify and resolve run-on sentences:

Incorrect: It is so hot today I think I will visit the swimming pool and then take a nap.

Correct: It is so hot today. I think I will visit the swimming pool and then take a nap.

Incorrect: You couldn't possibly have done that yourself, did your friends help you?

Correct: You couldn't possibly have done that yourself. Did your friends help you?

3.2.3 Avoid Beginning Sentences with but, and, also, and so

It is best to avoid beginning sentences with the words *but*, *and*, *also*, and *so*. *But*, *and*, and *so* are coordinating conjunctions whose function is to connect elements of equal rank within a sentence. Likewise, *also* is an adverb, occasionally used as a subordinating conjunction to connect two clauses of unequal rank (i.e. dependent clause and independent clause). Rather than using these words at the beginning of a sentence, we can connect the adjacent clauses into one sentence. Alternatively, we may employ adverbial conjunctions such as *however*, *nevertheless*, *moreover*, etc., whose function it is to connect independent clauses. (This is also dealt with later in the chapter in the section introducing clauses). Consider the examples below:

Incorrect: Frederick wanted to go. ***But*** he was told to stay behind.

Correct: Frederick wanted to go, ***but*** he was told to stay behind.

Correct: Frederick wanted to go. ***Nonetheless***, he was told to stay behind.

Incorrect: We swept and mopped the floor. ***Also***, we washed the dishes.

Correct: We swept and mopped the floor ***and*** washed the dishes.

Correct: We swept and mopped the floor. We ***also*** washed the dishes. (Here we employ *also* as an adverb instead of a conjunction.)

3.2.4 Adjectives and Adjective Clauses

Adjectives modify nouns or pronouns and typically appear in front of the word they describe. Examples include "*yellow* hat," "*best* friend," and "*great* party." Adjective clauses modify nouns or pronouns as do single-word adjectives, but follow after the word and are introduced either by a relative pronoun (*who*, *whose*, *whom*, *which*, *that*) or by a subordinating conjunction (*where*, *when*, or *why*). Examples include "the hat *that I bought last week,*" "the friend *who I met at the diner*," and "the party *where the clown entertained the children*." As a general rule, if the modifier (in English) contains a verb, we must use an adjective clause that follows the verb.

3.2.5 Avoid Double Negatives

As the term suggests, a double negative occurs when two negative and opposing ideas appear in the same sentence:

I *didn't not* want to go.
Tom *didn't* see *no* one at the park.

The effective meanings of these sentences are:

I *did* want to go.
Tom *did* see someone at the park.

If the negative meaning is intended, these sentences must be rewritten using a single negative. Often trouble occurs when both the verb is negated and the object is replaced with a negative pronoun. In such a case, either one or the other will suffice.

Correct: I *did not* want to go.
Correct: Tom *didn't* see anyone at the park. (negative verb, positive pronoun)
Correct: Tom saw *no* one at the park. (positive verb, negative pronoun)

3.2.6 Avoid Dangling Participles

Participial phrases begin with a verb in the –ing form and modify nouns as in the following examples:

John, *knowing that his girlfriend was coming over,* cleaned his apartment.
Forgetting to wipe his prints off the glass, the burglar was soon identified.

Participial phrases must be placed in close proximity to the word they are modifying. Dangling participles are participial phrases located at a distance from the noun they intend to modify. As shown in the examples below, these confusing sentences can be clarified by relocating the participial phrase or by altogether rephrasing the modifier.

Incorrect: *Spurting gas all the way*, Otis slowly drove his car into town. (It is unclear what is spurting gas, Otis or his car.)

Correct: Otis slowly drove his car, spurting gas all the way, into town.

Correct: Otis slowly drove his car into town as it spurted gas all the way.

Incorrect: Hanging in the belfry, a monk rang the church bell three times. (It is unclear who or what is hanging in the belfry, the monk or the bell.)

Correct: A monk rang the church bell hanging in the belfry three times.

Correct: A monk rang the church bell that hangs in the belfry three times.

3.2.7 Avoid Postponed Prepositions

A postponed preposition is one that appears after its object. This is usually done because the proper construction is self-referential, wordy, and seems less natural. In this case the writer has three options: using the formal construction as it is preferred in academic writing even if it may seem awkward; using the informal and perhaps more natural version; or rephrasing the sentence entirely. To convert the informal to formal requires rearranging the sentence so that the preposition occurs in front of its object, and then employing a relative pronoun (*who*, *whom*, *which*, etc.) that serves as the object of the preposition. A preferable option is to rewrite the syntax of the sentence entirely, wherein we construct an ordinary prepositional phrase that does not reference itself. In summary our options are to:

1. Opt for the incorrect but more natural sounding version
2. Rearrange the position of the preposition, add relative pronoun
3. Rephrase the entire syntax of the sentence

The sentences below give examples of all three:

Informal: That is the friend I gave my watch *to*.
Formal: That is the friend *to whom* I gave my watch.
Rephrased: I gave my watch to that friend.
Informal: There is the police officer I spoke *with*.
Formal: There is the police officer *with whom* I spoke.
Rephrased: I spoke with that police officer.

3.3 Sentences

All complete sentences contain a core of a subject married to a predicate. The subject is the person or thing being written about. The predicate describes what the writer wishes to convey about the subject. Consider the sentence *Manchester United lost the game.* **Manchester United** is the subject, and the verb **lost** is the predicate. If a sentence does not contain both of these concepts it is incomplete. This particular sentence also contains the object **the game**. Many sentences will include an object – the thing or person to which the subject's feelings or actions relate. *I love you* is perhaps the simplest and most famous example of subject, predicate, and object. This simple core of a sentence can be expanded in one of two ways. First, we can add modifiers to the subject, predicate, and/or object; second, we can join two or more such simple sentences (or clauses) together to form a multi-clausal sentence.

3.3.1 Modifiers

Modifiers add further information to a sentence to describe the situation in a more accurate or more pleasing way. We can modify the subject: *The **Evil** Empire struck back.* We can modify the verb: *I **really** love you.* We can modify the object: *Manchester United lost the **most important** game **of the season**.* If we modify all three elements, the sentence will of course be far from the simple clause with which we started. However, sometimes modifiers are less closely related to the individual elements of the core, and are of such length as to require separation from the core by commas.

We can add lengthy modifiers before the core such as in the sentence: ***After coming back from a three-nil deficit,*** *Liverpool went on to win the Champions League.* We can add information inside the core: *Vladimir Smicer, **in his last game for the club,** brought Liverpool to within a single goal.* Finally, we can add such modifiers after the core such as in the sentence: *We will move house, **as soon as the renovations are completed*** (Pearsall and Cunningham 1998, 132-133). The importance of the comma in these, and in much longer sentences, is apparent. Not only does it serve to give clarification of meaning, it also gives the reader a chance to "breathe."

Effective use of commas can allow the construction (and understanding by the reader) of quite lengthy sentences. However, in general, it is a good idea to get to the core of the sentence fairly quickly, otherwise the reader will have to retain too much information in their head before they get to the central meaning. In addition, it is important to avoid separating the elements of the core with too many addition words. Finally, while long sentences often look impressive, and in some cases are necessary, in general it is often better to break such sentences up into shorter distinct sentences in order to aid comprehension. Remember, in academic writing one is attempting to convey information in the most convincing way possible, rather than trying to confuse the reader.

3.3.2 Clauses

The sentence core described above can, in some cases, form only one of two or more distinct clauses in a sentence. Each clause must contain, at the least, a subject and a verb. In this section we will consider how to link clauses in multi-clausal sentences. There are two kinds of clauses: independent and dependent. The independent clause is a complete thought, one that could in itself form a stand-alone sentence. The core sentences discussed above are good examples of independent clauses. Dependent clauses do not form complete thoughts, and cannot stand alone as sentences. An example of a dependent clause is: *...if North Korea tests its nuclear weapons....* Clearly this clause needs another clause to either precede or follow it in order to form a complete sentence.

Two or more clauses can be linked in a single sentence through what are known as clause connectors. There are three types of clause connectors: subordinators (subordinating conjunctions), coordinators (coordinating conjunctions), and conjunctive adverbs (Oshima and Hogue 1999, 153). Subordinators often (although not always) come at the start of a multi-clausal sentence, and make one clause dependent or subordinate to another. Examples of subordinators include: *after, although, as soon as, because, before, even though, if, since, that, when, whenever, where, wherever, which,* and etc. A multi-clausal sentence within which a dependent clause is linked to an independent clause by a subordinator is called a complex sentence.

Adverbs that form subordinators (sometimes called adverbial subordinators) can be divided into a number of different groups. The first type links one clause to another by telling you why whatever occurred or will occur happened. Examples of such adverbial subordinators include *because, since,* and *as*. ***Since*** *you refuse to behave yourself, you will not be allowed to go to the party*. The second type tells you when or where whatever occurred happened or will happen. Examples include *after, as soon as, before, since, when, whenever, where, wherever,* and etc. ***As soon as*** *you finish your homework, you can watch television.* The third type introduces an opposing idea. Examples include *although, even though,* and *though.* ***Even though*** *an armistice brought an end to the fighting on the Korean peninsula a long time ago, the two sides remain technically at war*.

Coordinators usually form a link between two independent clauses and occur in the middle of multi-clausal sentences. There are seven coordinators: *for, and, nor, but, or, yet, so*. In general it is best, in academic writing, to avoid placing coordinators at the beginning of sentences. Although creative writing allows a sentence to begin with And or But for emphasis, this practice is frowned upon by some academics, and therefore should be avoided if for no other reason than the desire to maintain a sympathetic audience for your work. Multi-clausal sentences within which two distinct clauses are linked by a coordinator are called compound sentences. The following is an example of a compound sentence: *He is quite old for a singer,* ***but*** *he still has a good voice*.

Finally, there are many conjunctive adverbs, including: *accordingly, besides, consequently, for example, furthermore, hence, however, in addition, indeed, nevertheless, nevertheless, on the other hand, therefore, thus*, and etc. Conjunctive adverbs give us additional information related to the initial statement, either reinforcing it or contradicting it. Conjunctive adverbs can be used to link clauses in multi-clausal sentences. However, they can also be used to link distinct sentences, as is the case with the link between this sentence and the preceding one.

3.3.3 Using Clause Connectors

Our example of a dependent clause (above) uses the subordinator *if*. To form a multi-clausal sentence we could add another clause either before or after the dependent clause: 1) ***If*** *North Korea tests its nuclear weapons, the United States will declare war.* 2) *Japan will be very worried* ***if*** *North Korea tests its nuclear weapons.* A coordinator can also be used to link two or more clauses in a similar way: *a weak national currency can stimulate exports,* ***but*** *it will make imports more costly.* In all these cases, the comma is used strategically to enhance comprehension and ease of reading.

However, with regard to conjunctive adverbs, the comma is not the only grammatical device that can be used. As already mentioned, conjunctive adverbs can be used to link two distinct sentences. In addition, these adverbs can be used in conjunction with semicolons to link two independent clauses: *North Korean nuclear testing will greatly alarm the United States;* ***nevertheless,*** *war is unlikely.* Note that in this case the conjunctive adverb follows the semicolon, and a comma follows the conjunctive adverb. Finally, clauses can be linked together by the simple use of a semicolon, without the explicit use of clause connectors. Consider: *Confucian family values are in decline; half of marriages end in divorce.*

3.3.4 Active Versus Passive Voice

Voice is the form a verb takes to indicate whether the subject of the sentence acts or is acted upon. Consider: *The victorious Allies liberated Paris.* Versus: *Paris was liberated by the victorious Allies.* Both these forms are grammatically correct. However, in English (unlike some other languages), and particularly in academic English, active voice is generally preferred. This is because passive voice can lead to long, complicated sentences. Usually we are explaining what does what to what; therefore it makes sense to place the actor before the action and the action before the object (Pearsall and Cunningham 1998, 139). In addition, whereas at times the passive voice might sound more elegant, in academic English writing we are trying to sound precise and scientific, and for this the active voice performs better. We should use the passive voice only when we are deliberately trying to emphasize the importance of the object over the subject. For instance: *The United Nations Charter* ***was signed*** *by the participants of the San Francisco conference.*

3.4 Paragraphs

Simply put, a paragraph is a collection of sentences. More specifically, a paragraph serves to direct the reader to a collection of related ideas contained in a group of sentences. The number of sentences in the group may vary, just as the number of clauses in a sentence, or the length of sentences themselves may vary. However, research has demonstrated that the average English language paragraph contains five to ten sentences with 75 to 150 words (Rooks 1999, 6). Paragraphs form the building blocks of much larger compositions, from telegrams through academic essays, up to and including theses or books. The relationships between paragraphs within some of these larger compositions are dealt with in Chapter 4. In this chapter we will address the relationship and purposes of sentences within paragraphs.

Standard paragraphs usually begin with a statement of the main idea, point or question being addressed. The rest of the paragraph then serves to illustrate the main point, to further develop it, to supply supporting evidence, and / or to get down to specifics. Finally, the paragraph should conclude with something of a summary with regard to the collection of ideas that have been addressed. Unrelated matter should not be addressed, but should, if relevant to the larger discourse of the writing, be included in a separate paragraph. These rules have been formulated into a widely accepted structure for academic paragraph writing. In general a paragraph should have a topic statement (one sentence), subject development (comprising three to eight sentences), and a summary (usually a single sentence).

3.4.1 Topic Statements

A topic statement must clearly express the main topic, idea or theme of the paragraph which is to be addressed by the following sentences. It must seize the attention of the reader, or else the content of the rest of the paragraph may not be absorbed, and the paragraph will be passed over in a most cursory manner. The topic statement often appears as the first sentence of a paragraph, and helps structure the direct logical development of arguments. In addition to identifying the central point to be developed, the topic statement will often bring up any potential clashes or contending points of view. In a longer piece of work, the topic statement may also provide useful "signposting," linking the paragraph with preceding discussions, and will communicate the specific parts of a larger general subject addressed by the work that will be developed in the paragraph.

Consider for example the topic statement: *In recent years the United States has made increasing calls upon its allies to shoulder a fairer share of the burden of world leadership.* We know that the paragraph is going to address the requests for contributions from other countries towards the costs that the United States incurs in its leadership role. However, the wider subject addressed by the work as a whole, might be that of declining US hegemony or world leadership. Appeals to allies for help have long been associated in the literature with such a condition.

3.4.2 Subject Development

Once the subject matter to be covered by the paragraph has been correctly and accurately identified by the topic statement, the ensuing sentences may develop this matter in two different ways: subject development sentences may include explanatory statements, or they may include illustrative statements. Explanatory statements aid comprehension of the relationships between concepts within the paragraph and between the paragraph and other paragraphs or the wider piece of work. They serve to clarify what exactly this paragraph is dealing with in the wider context of the general argument. They give theoretical structure to the evaluation of the abstract concept contained within the topic statement. Illustrative statements aid comprehension of, and add conviction to, the theoretical concepts addressed by the paragraph. This may be done through giving concrete, real-world examples of the points raised, through citing facts, statistics or individual experience, or by quoting or paraphrasing the comments of others on the topic, particularly if these others are considered experts in the field.

3.4.3 Summaries

Like the topic statement sentence of a paragraph, the summary sentence performs a vital role in giving weight and structure to the paragraph as a whole. The summary sentence must punctuate and underline what has been said in the paragraph. If the summary sentence makes no impact upon the reader, it is likely that the contents of the paragraph will soon be forgotten. In addition, the summary performs a vital signposting function, linking the paragraph to surrounding paragraphs and to the wider piece of work. The summary sentence should not only recap what has been discussed in the paragraph, but also stimulate further thinking on the part of the reader.

There are a number of ways in which a summary sentence can be constructed. First, it can refer back to the topic statement, demonstrating how the subject development has answered or addressed any questions raised in the opening sentence. Second, it can form a logical conclusion based on the flow of evidence addressed in the subject development sentences. Third, it can repeat the main ideas of the paragraph in a new and eye-catching way. Fourth, and finally, it can explicitly link or signpost the contribution of the paragraph to a wider discussion or thematic development in the piece of academic work.

3.4.4 Creating Structural Links Within Paragraphs

As mentioned above, all the sentences within a single paragraph must be related to a single topic. Matter that is not closely related to the topic must be excluded from the paragraph. In order to demonstrate the close relationship between each of the sentences in the paragraph and the topic, and also the close relationship between the individual sentences, it is necessary to link each sentence to those preceding and following it. We use sentence connectors to perform this function. Sentence connectors occur in two forms: continuing connectors, and transition connectors. Every paragraph should have a number of each of these types of connectors, and each sentence should explicitly be linked to the overall structure of the paragraph through them.

Continuing connectors are used when the discussion in a particular sentence concerns the same subject as that found in the preceding sentence. That is to say that subject "continues." There are three kinds of continuing connectors: repeated words and phrases, demonstrative adjectives, and pronouns (Rooks 1999, 37). With regard to repeated words or phrases, consider the following: *A society without government is considered to be in a* ***state of anarchy****. A* ***state of anarchy*** *may be viewed as a war of all against all.* Demonstrative adjectives include this, that, these and those. Consider: *The five Permanent members of the United Nations Security Council are the United Kingdom, the United States, China, France, and Russia.* ***These*** *Members are also called the Veto holders.* The following is an example of a pronoun as a continuing connector: ***They*** *are given the power to block any resolutions they consider contrary to their interests.*

Transition connectors are used when the subject of a particular sentence is not the same as that found in the preceding sentence, as it has been significantly modified, expanded, narrowed, or otherwise changed. Transition connectors serve to identify the relationship between the subjects in linked sentences. In other words, they perform the "transition" from one subject to another. George Rooks (1999, 38) has identified 9 major transitional relationships between sentences: 1) consequence (result); 2) comparison (likeness); 3) contrast (difference); 4) example (illustration); 5) restatement (repetition); 6) addition; 7) concession (even though); 8) sequence (order); 9) summary (conclusion).

A consequential relationship between sentences occurs when the subject mater in a sentence can be seen to have been caused, to be a consequence of, or to logically follow from the material presented in the preceding sentence(s). Such a sentence will typically begin with the transition connectors *therefore*, *thus*, or *as a result*. *China's economy has been growing at a phenomenal rate for the last 20 years.* ***Therefore****, it is likely to overtake the economy of the United States in terms of scale by the year 2050.* Comparisons occur when the matter in a sentence is either similar in itself or addressed in a similar way to the matter in another sentence. Such sentences begin with *likewise*, *similarly*, or *in the same way*. *Smoking can have a detrimental effect on performance by reducing lung capacity.* ***In the same way****, excessive alcohol intake can reduce performance through contributing to weight-gain.* A contrasting relationship occurs when matter is treated in a different way in subsequent sentences. Examples include: *however*, *on the contrary*, *on the other hand*, and *conversely*. *There is no global government.* ***However****, this does not mean that there is not international order.*

Example, restatement and addition transition connectors expand upon the conceptual matter examined in preceding sentences. Examples may often serve to clarify a preceding statement using the connectors *for example*, or *for instance*. *She is always so greedy and selfish.* ***For instance****, last night she ate all the pizza before I came home.* Restatements are often preceded with the transition connector *in other words*. *North Korea is considered a rogue regime.* ***In other words****, it does not follow the rules and laws of international society.* Addition connectors simply add further matter on a related subject to that presented in preceding sentences, they include *in addition*, *also*, *moreover*, and *furthermore*. *Drug use during pregnancy has been* *demonstrated to pose serious threats to the unborn child's future development.* ***In addition****, it dramatically increases the chances of a miscarriage.*

Concessions are used when, despite previous statements to the contrary, the contrasting evidence in the sentence is still considered very important. Such sentences often begin with *nevertheless*, or *nonetheless. The Soviet Union greatly restricted the freedoms of its citizens.* ***Nevertheless****, in present-day Russia there is still a degree of nostalgia for the certainties of the old days*. Sequences of sentences occur in the form of *first, second, third...* or *to begin with, next, after, finally/lastly*. Summaries bring together the information from preceding sentences. Examples include: *in conclusion*, *to summarize*, and *in summary*.

3.4.5 Paragraph Outline

The outline of a standard paragraph might look like the following:

A. **Topic sentence/statement**
B. *Subject development sentence.*
C. Explanatory and illustrative statements linked by continuing connectors.
D. *Subject development sentence introduced with transition connector.*
E. Explanatory and illustrative statements linked to second subject development sentence by continuing connectors.
F. *Subject development sentence introduced with transition connector.*
G. Explanatory and illustrative statements linked to third subject development sentence by continuing connectors.

H. Concluding sentence/summary

In this outline the subject development sentences are the main points of the paragraph, and support the overall topic of the paragraph introduced by the topic sentence. Each of the subject development sentences is supported with explanatory and illustrative statements. The concluding sentence or summary refers back to how the topic introduced at the start has been developed throughout the paragraph (Oshima and Hogue 1997, 83).

While it is unlikely that any writer will formally map out each and every paragraph in this fashion, it is nevertheless a good idea to have such a model in the back of your mind when writing. At the very least, it is a good idea to put down the major points of each paragraph in "bullet" form before writing your larger piece of academic work, in order to make sure that all the points that fall under a single topic are grouped together, and that no paragraph contains incongruous material (matter that does not fit with the other major points or with the larger topic as a whole).

3.5 Summary

Sentences and paragraphs form the main building blocks of academic writing. Each sentence is made up of one or more clauses; each paragraph is made up of a number of sentences. There are rules regulating the construction of sentences and the linkage of sentences within paragraphs. Following these rules allows both clearer and more convincing expression of ideas, as well as making the reading experience easier and more enjoyable.

Sentences may be simple, complex, or compound. In a simple sentence, a subject is married to a predicate (verb), and in most sentences an object is also included. Each of these elements can be expanded through the addition of modifiers. In addition, we can add lengthy modifiers before, inside, or after the core. A complex sentence is a multi-clausal sentence within which one clause is made subordinate to or dependent on another by a subordinator. A compound sentence is a multi-clausal sentence within which a coordinator forms a link between two or more independent clauses. Finally, two or more clauses (or sentences) can be linked together using conjunctive adverbs.

Paragraphs are made up of a number of sentences (5-10 sentences, 75-150 words) on a related theme. Unrelated matter should not be included in the paragraph. Each paragraph should consist of a topic statement (one sentence), subject development (comprising three to eight sentences), and a summary (usually a single sentence). Sentences within each paragraph should be linked through a combination of continuing connectors, and transition connectors. Continuing connectors are used when the subject matter continues from one sentence to the next. There are three kinds of continuing connectors: repeated words and phrases, demonstrative adjectives, and pronouns. Transition connectors are used when the subject matter changes from one sentence to the next. The different types of transitional relationships between sentences are: 1) consequence (result); 2) comparison (likeness); 3) contrast (difference); 4) example (illustration); 5) restatement (repetition); 6) addition; 7) concession (even though); 8) sequence (order); 9) summary (conclusion).

The following chapter will demonstrate how to develop links between paragraphs in larger pieces of academic writing

References

Oshima, Alice and Ann Hogue. 1997. *Introduction to Academic Writing: Second Edition.* White Plains, NY: Addison Wesley Longman.

Oshima, Alice and Ann Hogue. 1999. *Writing Academic English: Third Edition.* White Plains, NY: Addison Wesley Longman.

Pearsall, Thomas E. and Donald H. Cunningham. 1998. *The Fundamentals of Good Writing.* New York: Macmillan.

Rooks, George M. 1999. *Paragraph Power: Second Edition.* White Plains, NY: Pearson Education.

Chapter 4 The Academic Essay

4.1 Introduction

This chapter will address the most common form of academic writing, the essay. An academic essay is a relatively short piece of work (short enough to be read at a single sitting), that conveys an informed opinion about a single topic. It is not meant to be an all-encompassing treatment of the material. Rather, it is meant to give our opinion about an interesting part of the material.

In writing an essay, it is important at all times to remember that its purpose is to communicate something to the reader. Usually the purpose of this communication for a student writing an academic essay, will be to demonstrate to the reader (professor, tutor, examiner, etc.) comprehension of material covered in class and in readings, from an individual perspective. It is the student's "take" on the material, her attempt to condense some meaningful aspect of all that has been covered into a single, short piece of writing. That is why essay also means "try."

An essay is an organized discussion of a subject made up of a series of paragraphs (usually a minimum of four). Just as sentences and paragraphs have structure, so to do essays. There are a number of different acceptable essay structures, some of which will be dealt with in this chapter. However, whatever the structure, there are similar rules for organization, certain objectives that the essay must achieve, and different functions for different paragraphs within the essay. Just as within each paragraph there are certain specialized sentences with specific jobs to do, so too within each essay there are certain specialized paragraphs with specific jobs.

In this chapter, we will consider relatively simple academic essays. Longer pieces of work, such as research papers, dissertations, and theses follow many of the same rules, but involve added levels of complexity (most importantly elements of research and referencing) which are covered in Chapter 5 on research and Chapter 6 on citation. Here we will focus on the basic structure and functions of the academic essay. The next three sections will address the three constitutive parts of the essay: introduction; body; conclusion. The rest of the chapter will introduce the balanced essay, different ways in which paragraphs can be organized to fulfill these structural roles, and an overview of objectives.

4.2 The Introduction/Introductory Paragraphs

A good introductory paragraph will explain to the reader, about which part, of a wider body of knowledge, the author intends to write. This has often, and rather simplistically, been stated as "say what you are going to say." A more detailed and more useful checklist of what should go into an introduction focuses on what it is that you wish to communicate to your reader. Basically, you need to get the attention of the reader. You need not only to say what it is you are trying to convey or demonstrate, but also how this fits into the wider body of literature on the subject. You need to say how you are intending to support what it is you wish to demonstrate, and using which resources. Finally, you need to give a preview of what is to come in the main body of your essay.

Opinion is divided whether at this point it is necessary to state what your ultimate findings will be. One school of thought argues for a suspense approach with a triumphant reveal at the end of your essay. However, given that you are trying to communicate with the reader (and convince the examiner of your knowledge) in the clearest and most effective way, it is probably best to be transparent right from the start. The writer should provide "signposts" for the reader to help guide them through the arguments and evidence in the essay, and there is no good reason why this should not begin in the introduction. If the reader knows her ultimate destination, it may well be easier to see where the path is leading. If this process is not followed, early pieces of information could be overlooked by the reader, forgotten, or may even irritate the reader as she does not see the relevance of their introduction.

Thus, an introduction should provide the blueprint for what is to follow in the rest of the essay. This is not only to make it easier for the reader to follow, but also to make it easier to write the rest of the essay. Essentially, the rest of the essay fills in the gaps and expands upon what is stated in the introduction, even if the introduction usually only consists of a single paragraph. At the same time, the introduction should be kept as short and pithy as possible. The introduction is the first chance to impress a reader, and should not be undermined by irrelevant material or "waffle."

To conclude, the introduction should include:

- A "hook" or attention-grabbing sentence;
- A statement of purpose – what you are going to write about;
- A contextual summary – why this is an important topic;
- A thesis statement – what you are hoping to demonstrate;

- A preview of the body – what evidence and arguments you will use to support your thesis;
- A preview of your findings.

4.3 The Body

In the simplest terms, the body of your essay "says what you want to say." It is the substantive component of the essay, by far the longest part, and contains not only all the evidence used to back up your argument, but also the bulk of the analysis of this evidence. The body of your essay should contain a minimum of two paragraphs, and often contain far more than this, depending on the length of the essay, whereas both the introduction and the conclusion should generally be kept to a single paragraph each.

Each body paragraph should be related to the main theme of the essay as laid out in the introduction. If a body paragraph is not directly related to the main thrust of the argument being advanced and developed, it may well be that the paragraph is redundant, or that the introductory paragraph is too restrictive, and doesn't really convey what is intended. As mentioned in the previous chapter, each paragraph in the body should cover a distinct concept, and should contain all the material within the essay relating to that concept. However, each paragraph of the body should also explicitly be linked to neighboring paragraphs and to the conceptual whole of the larger essay.

Body paragraphs follow most closely the guidelines for paragraph construction outlined in Chapter 3. It is possible in some ways to view each body paragraph as an essay in miniature, as each contains an introduction, body, and conclusion. Naturally, each body paragraph will begin with a topic statement outlining the particular aspect of the essay's theme being addressed. This paragraph "introduction" should also link to the main theme and, if it is not the first body paragraph, could also contain a signpost linking it with a preceding paragraph.

The subject development described in Chapter 3 forms the "body" of each body paragraph. In this part of each body paragraph, explanatory and illustrative sentences of evidence combine with *comment* sentences explaining why the evidence is part of the *argument* being developed. The argument should run throughout the essay and form a unifying thematic link. It may help to explicitly link each body paragraph's topic to the central argument. If you are unable to do so it is likely that you have more than one argument in your essay, or, in fact, more than one essay masquerading as a single entity. This state of affairs is to be avoided. Keeping things simple will aid comprehension of your essay by the reader and that this, after all, is the point for which you are striving.

The summary or concluding sentences of body paragraphs may perform a number of the functions, as detailed in the preceding chapter. They can refer back to the topic statement; form logical conclusions based on the flow of evidence addressed in the subject development sentences; can repeat the main ideas of the paragraph in a new and eye-catching way; and/or can explicitly link or signpost the contribution of the paragraph to the essay as a whole. In addition, the summary of each body paragraph (except for the one immediately preceding the conclusion) must provide a transition to the next paragraph.

4.4 The Conclusion/Concluding Paragraphs

Like the introductory paragraph, the concluding paragraph of an academic essay performs a vital role. While the introduction is the first thing the reader comes across, and thus one of the functions of the introduction is to seize the attention of the reader; it is the conclusion that will leave a lasting impression in the mind of the reader, being the last thing she reads. If you have followed the rules for writing an essay up to this point, the conclusion should be the culmination of a process of logical thought progression beginning with the ideas laid out in the introduction, which were then developed in the body, and are now to be summed up in the final paragraph of the essay. Essentially the conclusion "says what you have said."

Indeed, much of the conclusion is a restatement of the introduction (although in different words, with a different emphasis and in a briefer form). In a similar way to the introduction, it will address the main thesis that was tested in the body, and also like the introduction, it will track the development of the argument throughout the essay. Just as the introduction should begin with a hook, so, also, the conclusion should end with a strong and memorable statement. However, the conclusion must also perform a number of other functions that in fact make it one of the trickiest parts of the essay to get right.

In addition to restating the argument, the conclusion needs to demonstrate how all of the evidence (or at least how on balance the weight of evidence) addressed in the body supports the argument. The conclusion also needs to place this argument in a wider contextual framework, pointing out how these findings differ from what might be expected, or from what others have claimed, or even how they agree with the writings of others and thus reinforce the claims of a particular school of thought. In essays where you have been given a question to answer, or where you have set up a hypothesis to test, the conclusion must state firmly how the essay as a whole has performed this task.

There are also certain elements that should not go into a conclusion. A conclusion must not bring up new topics, evidence or discussions that have not already been addressed in the body of the essay. If this material is relevant to the central argument of the essay it should be addressed in the body and only then referred to in the conclusion. If it is not relevant to the central argument of the essay it should be excluded from the whole essay, and in particular from the conclusion, as it will only serve to confuse the reader by blurring your central message. This is the exact opposite of what you are hoping to achieve with the conclusion which in many cases serves to provide order out of chaos.

Finally, a conclusion must not make absurd generalized claims. Your essay will have only drawn upon limited evidence and analyzed only specific cases, therefore your findings can only be applied in a limited way. You will not have addressed all the concepts related to the topic in the body of your (short) essay, and will not have provided all the answers to all the problems, thus you must be careful with any claims you make (Mounsey 2002, 40-41).

For instance, even if, in analyzing the brutal conquest of one country by another, you are able to demonstrate that the leadership of the aggressor had scant regard for civilian suffering, you cannot generalize solely from that evidence that such tendencies apply to all people from that country in all periods of history. In fact, it would probably not even be possible to generalize to other sections of the aggressor's society during the timeframe considered. The only generalization that could possibly be made is that there existed a culture within the leadership of that country at that time, which took a disdainful attitude towards civilians in general, and enemy civilians in particular.

Having analyzed the constitutive elements of a simple essay, we will now turn to consider some more advanced structures for academic essay writing. In particular, the following sections will address the vital concept of the balanced essay, and give models of paragraph structures that will best reflect balance in your work.

4.5 The Balanced Essay

The simple essay described above has a structure with a single paragraph for introduction, two or three paragraphs of body, each with a topic that essentially supports the central argument, followed by a single concluding paragraph demonstrating how each of the body paragraphs have supported the central argument with evidence and analysis, thus proving the central hypothesis. However, such a degree of simplification is often not sufficient for an academic essay. Most of the time, the line of argument you are pursuing in your essay is only one of many possible interpretations of the evidence. You may think that it is the strongest one, nevertheless it is important to consider competing theories. When more than one competing theory or explanation is considered in a single essay, it is important to know how to structure the arguments and provide balance between them. This is the balanced essay.

There are two main reasons why it is important to get balance in an academic essay. First and foremost, in writing an academic essay you are trying to give at least the appearance of objectivity to your reader. Rather than simply extolling the virtues of one side while ignoring contradictory interpretations of the other, it is far more convincing in scientific terms to say that having considered both sides of the argument (and being able to demonstrate active consideration of both sides) you feel that on balance of the evidence, one side is more convincing than the other. Your conclusion can then be portrayed as a judgement based on the evidence rather than mere personal opinion (although of course it will always be a judgement slanted in favor of the argument you are promoting – a biased adjudication).

Second, by addressing contrary evidence and interpretations of this evidence within your own essay, you can to a certain extent draw the sting from any criticism of your argument. This can be thought of as immunizing your reader against criticisms of your position that may be brought by those supporting opposing approaches. The best way to do this is to identify what the arguments might be that could be coming to challenge you, then introduce these arguments in a weaker form in order to rebut them in your essay.

It is particularly important to take this approach when writing an academic essay that will be marked or examined. If you, as the author, have not addressed contradictory positions and evidence within your essay, throughout the evaluation procedure the examiner will be thinking of everything you have omitted. Not only will this lose you marks for submitting an incomplete treatment of the subject, it may also prejudice the reader in the direction of the omitted arguments – precisely the opposite of the biased adjudication for which you were hoping.

4.6 Structuring the Academic Essay

The simple academic essay described above can be modeled in the following way:

Figure 1. Simple Academic Essay Structure

<table>
<tr><td>

INTRODUCTION

- "Hook" or attention grabbing sentence.
- Statement of purpose – what you are going to write about.
- Contextual summary – why this is an important topic.
- Thesis statement – what you are hoping to demonstrate.
- Preview of the body – what evidence and arguments you will use to support your thesis.
- Preview of your findings.

</td></tr>
<tr><td>

BODY PARAGRAPH 1

- Topic statement – main idea of the paragraph, linked to central theme or argument of the essay as a whole.
- Subject development - explanatory and illustrative sentences of evidence combined with *comment* sentences explaining why the evidence is part of the *argument* being developed.
- Summary – should also include a transition or signpost linking it to the next paragraph.

</td></tr>
<tr><td>

BODY PARAGRAPH 2

- Topic statement – main idea of the paragraph, linked to central theme or argument of the essay as a whole. May also include a link back to previous paragraph.
- Subject development – explanatory and illustrative sentences of evidence combined with *comment* sentences explaining why the evidence is part of the *argument* being developed.
- Summary – should also include a transition or signpost linking it to the next paragraph.

</td></tr>
<tr><td>

BODY PARAGRAPH 3

- Topic statement – main idea of the paragraph, linked to central theme or argument of the essay as a whole. May also include a link back to previous paragraph(s).
- Subject development – explanatory and illustrative sentences of evidence combined with *comment* sentences explaining why the evidence is part of the *argument* being developed.
- Summary.

</td></tr>
<tr><td>

CONCLUSION

- Thesis restatement.
- Summary of evidence and argument presented.
- Brief contextual analysis.
- Strong statement.

</td></tr>
</table>

As might be expected, the balanced essay requires a more complex model. Structure is in fact even more important in the balanced essay. Not only must care be taken that each paragraph addresses only a single topic, and that all related material goes into that paragraph, but also that related arguments are grouped together, or occur in the same order throughout the essay.

There are two basic ways we can go about organizing a balanced essay. The first model starts with the evidence and arguments that contradict the main hypothesis, then constructs stronger arguments supportive of the main hypothesis. This gives a paragraph structure of *Introduction, Negative Hypothesis Body 1, Negative Hypothesis Body 2, Positive Hypothesis Body 1, Positive Hypothesis Body 2, Conclusion.* The second model tackles each major issue in turn, first addressing the interpretations that contradict the hypothesis, then rebutting them with supportive interpretations. This gives a paragraph structure of *Introduction, Body Topic 1 (against and for), Body Topic 2 (against and for), Body Topic 3 (against and for), Body Topic 4 (against and for), [and etc.], Conclusion.* The second form is more suitable for longer essays where you have a lot of topics.

More sophisticated versions of these models may include rebuttal sections or paragraphs, and/or a third way between two competing hypotheses. The first of these moderations could yield structures such as: *Introduction, Negative Hypothesis Body, Rebuttal Body, Positive Hypothesis Body, Conclusion;* or *Introduction, Body Topic 1 (against, rebuttal and for), Body Topic 2 (against, rebuttal and for), Body Topic 3 (against, rebuttal and for), [and etc.], Conclusion.* The second moderation could yield structures such as: *Introduction, Hypothesis 1 Body, Rebuttal Body, Hypothesis 2, Rebuttal Body, Hypothesis 3 Body, Conclusion;* or *Introduction, Body Topic 1 (against, for, third way), Body Topic 2 (against, for, third way), Body Topic 3 (against, for, third way), [and etc.], Conclusion.*

The important thing to remember is that whichever approach you choose, you stick to it throughout the essay. The following are models of some of these approaches:

Figure 2. Balanced Essay [A]

INTRODUCTION
• "Hook" or attention grabbing sentence. • Statement of purpose – what you are going to write about. • Contextual summary – why this is an important topic, including conflicting arguments. • Thesis statement – what you are hoping to demonstrate. • Preview of the body – what evidence and arguments you will use to support your thesis. • Preview of your findings.
NEGATIVE HYPOTHESIS BODY PARAGRAPH
• Topic statement – main idea of the paragraph, linked to repudiation of the central theme or argument of the essay as a whole. • Subject development – explanatory and illustrative sentences of evidence combined with *comment* sentences explaining why the evidence contradicts the *argument* being developed. • Summary – should also include a transition or signpost linking it to the next paragraph.
REBUTTAL BODY PARAGRAPH
• Topic statement – main idea of the paragraph, including a link back to and rebuttal statement regarding previous paragraph. • Subject development – explanatory and illustrative sentences of evidence combined with *comment* sentences explaining why the evidence or argument presented previously is flawed. • Summary – should also include a transition or signpost linking it to the next paragraph.
POSITIVE HYPOTHESIS BODY PARAGRAPH
• Topic statement – main idea of the paragraph, linked to central theme or argument of the essay as a whole. May also include a link back to previous paragraph. • Subject development – explanatory and illustrative sentences of evidence combined with *comment* sentences explaining why the

evidence is part of the *argument* being developed.
• Summary – should also include why the argument of the positive hypothesis offers a better explanation of the evidence than that of the negative hypothesis.
CONCLUSION • Thesis restatement. • Summary of evidence and arguments presented. • Brief contextual analysis –summary of both sides. • Biased adjudication. • Strong statement.

Figure 3. Balanced Essay [B]

INTRODUCTION
• "Hook" or attention grabbing sentence. • Statement of purpose – what you are going to write about. • Contextual summary – why this is an important topic, including conflicting arguments. • Thesis statement – what you are hoping to demonstrate. • Preview of the body – what evidence and arguments you will use to support your thesis. • Preview of your findings.
BODY PARAGRAPH 1 • Topic statement – main idea of the paragraph, linked to the central theme or argument of the essay as a whole. • Subject development, counterhypothesis – explanatory and illustrative sentences of evidence combined with *comment* sentences explaining why the evidence contradicts the *argument* being developed. • Subject development, rebuttal – explanatory and illustrative sentences of evidence combined with *comment* sentences explaining why the evidence or argument presented previously is flawed. • Subject development, hypothesis - explanatory and illustrative sentences of evidence combined with *comment* sentences explaining why the evidence is part of the *argument* being developed. • Summary – review of why, based on analysis of the evidence, the positive hypothesis should be preferred to the counter-hypothesis with regard to the topic covered in this paragraph. Should also include a transition or signpost linking it to the next paragraph.

BODY PARAGRAPH 2

- Topic statement – main idea of the paragraph, linked to the central theme or argument of the essay as a whole. May also include a link back to previous paragraph.
- Subject development, counterhypothesis – explanatory and illustrative sentences of evidence combined with *comment* sentences explaining why the evidence contradicts the *argument* being developed.
- Subject development, rebuttal – explanatory and illustrative sentences of evidence combined with *comment* sentences explaining why the evidence or argument presented previously is flawed.
- Subject development, hypothesis - explanatory and illustrative sentences of evidence combined with *comment* sentences explaining why the evidence is part of the *argument* being developed.
- Summary – review of why, based on analysis of the evidence, the positive hypothesis should be preferred to the counter-hypothesis with regard to the topic covered in this paragraph. Should also include a transition or signpost linking it to the next paragraph.

BODY PARAGRAPH 3

- Topic statement – main idea of the paragraph, linked to the central theme or argument of the essay as a whole. May also include a link back to previous paragraph.
- Subject development, counterhypothesis – explanatory and illustrative sentences of evidence combined with *comment* sentences explaining why the evidence contradicts the *argument* being developed.
- Subject development, rebuttal – explanatory and illustrative sentences of evidence combined with *comment* sentences explaining why the evidence or argument presented previously is flawed.
- Subject development, hypothesis - explanatory and illustrative sentences of evidence combined with *comment* sentences explaining why the evidence is part of the *argument* being developed.
- Summary – review of why, based on analysis of the evidence, the positive hypothesis should be preferred to the counter-hypothesis with regard to the topic covered in this paragraph. Should also include a transition or signpost linking it to the next paragraph.

CONCLUSION

- Thesis restatement.
- Summary of evidence and arguments presented.
- Brief contextual analysis –summary of both sides.
- Biased adjudication.
- Strong statement.

Figure 4. Balanced Essay [C]

<table>
<tr><td>

INTRODUCTION

- "Hook" or attention grabbing sentence.
- Statement of purpose – what you are going to write about.
- Contextual summary – why this is an important topic, including conflicting arguments.
- Thesis statement – what you are hoping to demonstrate.
- Preview of the body – what evidence and arguments you will use to support your thesis.
- Preview of your findings.

</td></tr>
<tr><td>

FIRST HYPOTHESIS BODY PARAGRAPH

- Topic statement – main idea of the paragraph, linked to central theme or argument of the essay as a whole.
- Subject development – explanatory and illustrative sentences of evidence combined with *comment* sentences explaining why the evidence supports this interpretation.
- Summary – should also include a transition or signpost linking it to the next paragraph.

</td></tr>
<tr><td>

REBUTTAL BODY PARAGRAPH

- Topic statement – main idea of the paragraph, including a link back to and rebuttal statement regarding previous paragraph.
- Subject development – explanatory and illustrative sentences of evidence combined with *comment* sentences explaining why the evidence or argument presented previously is flawed.
- Summary – should also include a transition or signpost linking it to the next paragraph.

</td></tr>
<tr><td>

SECOND HYPOTHESIS BODY PARAGRAPH

- Topic statement – main idea of the paragraph, linked to central theme or argument of the essay as a whole.
- Subject development – explanatory and illustrative sentences of evidence combined with *comment* sentences explaining why the evidence supports this interpretation.
- Summary – should also include a transition or signpost linking it to the next paragraph.

</td></tr>
</table>

REBUTTAL BODY PARAGRAPH
• Topic statement – main idea of the paragraph, including a link back to and rebuttal statement regarding previous paragraph. • Subject development – explanatory and illustrative sentences of evidence combined with *comment* sentences explaining why the evidence or argument presented previously is flawed. • Summary – should also include a transition or signpost linking it to the next paragraph.
THIRD HYPOTHESIS BODY PARAGRAPH
• Topic statement – main idea of the paragraph, linked to central theme or argument of the essay as a whole. • Subject development – explanatory and illustrative sentences of evidence combined with *comment* sentences explaining why the evidence supports this interpretation. • Summary
CONCLUSION
• Thesis restatement. • Summary of evidence and arguments presented. • Brief contextual analysis –summary of all sides. • Biased adjudication. • Strong statement.

Once you are familiar with the internal paragraph structures of these models, for quick reference it may be convenient to think of them purely in terms of their paragraph headings, with each hypothesis and its supporting material only denoted by a letter. The various forms proposed above then become:

INTRODUCTION
B
B
A
A
CONCLUSION

INTRODUCTION
B A
B A
B A
CONCLUSION

INTRODUCTION
B
REBUTTAL
A
CONCLUSION

INTRODUCTION
B REBUTTAL A
B REBUTTAL A
B REBUTTAL A
CONCLUSION

INTRODUCTION
A
REBUTTAL
B
REBUTTAL
C
CONCLUSION

Whichever of these models you choose, or even should you choose a different variation of your own, that nevertheless provides a consistent and coherent structure to your essay, your argument or arguments should form a continuous thread throughout. The same structure should be followed at all times, and clear signposting adhered to in order to aid the reader's comprehension, and to contribute to a stronger case for the argument you are promoting as the most compelling. While it is not compulsory to always lead with the weaker argument, or the one that you hope to rebut, it is often in practice the easiest and most convincing approach to take.

4.7 Summary

Essays are the most common form of academic writing. They are composed of four or more linked paragraphs. All essays must contain an introduction or introductory paragraph, two or more body paragraphs, and a conclusion or concluding paragraph.

The introduction needs to get the attention of the reader; say what it is you are trying to convey or demonstrate and how this fits in the wider picture; have a thesis statement; and show how you are intending to support what it is you wish to demonstrate, and using which resources. It is the blueprint for your essay and needs to give a preview of what is to come.

The body must be made up of a number of paragraphs conceptually linked to the underlying argument and arranged in a logical and coherent way. Each body paragraph must have a clear topic statement, followed by explanatory and illustrative sentences of evidence combined with *comment* sentences developing the topic of the paragraph and central argument of the essay as a whole. Explicit signposting and transitions should link paragraphs to each other and contribute to the logical evolution of the essay.

The conclusion needs to come as a logical consequence of the preceding paragraphs. It should sum up what has gone before, not introduce any new material, answer any questions posed, refer back to the initial hypothesis, place the argument in a wider theoretical framework, and finish strongly.

The strongest form of the academic essays is the balanced essay. Balanced essays are more convincing as they appear more objective and reasoned, and also preempt criticism from opposing views. A number of different structures can be followed when constructing a balanced essay, but whichever is selected it must be followed throughout.

References

Mounsey, Chris. 2002. *Essays and Dissertations*. Oxford: Oxford University Press.

Chapter 5 Research and Research Paper Writing

5.1 Introduction

A student is often asked to prepare a research paper for his or her college courses. Generally, the assignment is given near the beginning of the semester, with the paper being due near the end. In such cases, it is generally understood that the instructor intends for the student to engage in the research process throughout the semester, thereby giving her time to investigate various resources, collect data, evaluate that which is most pertinent, contemplate her findings at length, and write a substantive paper. Unfortunately, many students overlook the importance of the *research* when writing a research paper. This chapter will outline the purposes of a research paper and a process that can be followed when preparing and writing the paper, regardless of its topic or length.

5.2 Purpose and Expectation

The writing process of a research paper is similar in design and style to that of an academic essay, as described in the previous chapter; however, the purpose of and preparation for a research paper differ somewhat significantly from the other types of writing. As the label indicates, the primary purpose is for the student to gain knowledge through research about a given topic, as an extension of, or outside that which is learned in the classroom. This is accomplished by initially exploring a broad variety of sources, eventually paring them down to those that are most pertinent to the subject matter the student wishes to explore in-depth, and then writing about one's new knowledge, often including summaries or direct quotes from the researched sources.

5.3 Choosing a Topic and Asking Questions

In some instances an instructor may provide an explicit topic to be studied, while at other times you will have a certain amount of freedom in choosing the focus of your research. In the latter case, you may be able to decide on a specific topic before you complete any in-depth research. However, it is more likely that you will be able to refine your subject matter through the course of your research. The most important component of any research project is **asking questions**. As Dieter Christensen, a wise mentor, regularly reminded his students, "If you do not learn to ask questions, you will never find any answers" (personal communication, n.d.). In other words, not only asking questions, but asking the right kinds of questions at the right time opens the door to true learning – an experience that will not only enable you to write a paper for a class assignment, but will also increase your wisdom and has the potential to enhance your life.

Jacqueline Berke and Randal Woodland (1994) suggest twenty questions a writer can use as he or she begins investigating a topic; an adaptation of their questions is listed below, along with the type of essay or research paper that might be generated from such questions. They are, of course, only preliminary questions to help get you started. Once you have narrowed down your research you will need to ask more specific questions related to your area of study.

Question	**Type of Answer**
1. What does X mean?	Definition
2. What are the various features of X?	Description
3. What are the components of X?	Simple Analysis
4. How is X made or done?	Process Analysis
5. How should X be made or done?	Directional Analysis
6. What is the essential function of X?	Functional Analysis
7. What are the causes of X?	Causal Analysis
8. What are the consequences of X?	Causal Analysis
9. What are the types of X?	Classification
10. How is X like or unlike Y?	Comparison
11. What is the present status of X?	Comparison
12. What is the significance of X?	Interpretation
13. What are the facts about X?	Reportage
14. How did X happen?	Narration
15. What kind of person is X?	Characterization
16. What is my personal response to X?	Reflection
17. What is my memory of X?	Reminiscence
18. What is the value of X?	Evaluation
19. What are the essential features of X?	Summary
20. What case can be made for or against X?	Persuasion

5.4 Doing the Research: Finding Information

As mentioned in the beginning of this chapter, the **research** aspect of a research paper is among the most significant portions of your work. Therefore, the bulk of this chapter will be devoted to finding, evaluating, and using resources.

Modern technology has opened the door to a wealth of electronic resources, many of which are valuable, but all of which must be properly evaluated in order to assess their quality and usefulness. Because of the ease of accessibility, many students begin their research using the Internet, which in general is perfectly acceptable. The problem lies in the fact that some students never go beyond the Internet to explore the wealth of information that exists in books, academic journals, indices, almanacs, atlases, newspapers, magazines, and government publications, guides and reports, among others. The Internet is a good place to start, and can be a resource for finding other sources, but never let it be the last or only arena of examination.

One should always visit the library (or libraries) when conducting research. Some libraries contain information related to a wide variety of topics, while others concentrate on only one subject (music, art, law, medicine, etc.). Libraries not only contain books and periodicals, but also make available a wide variety of other sources and information. For instance, in a Reference Room you will find sources that provide organized units of information such as dictionaries, encyclopedias, indexes, bibliographies, almanacs, statistics, directories, maps and college/university catalogs. The Periodical Room contains current issues of journals, magazines, and newspapers, as well as offers access to back issues. The A/V (Audio/Visual) Room provides use of videos, films, and DVDs, various forms of recordings (tapes, CDs, and LPs) as well as microfilm and microfiche. Many libraries also have special sections for rare books, special studies, and theses or dissertations, which should not be overlooked when conducting one's research.

Be aware, also, that certain governmental and civic organizations maintain records that may be useful to your studies, but which must often be read at a specific location. Be prepared, therefore, to take notes, and if possible make copies of all the information you need on the premises.

5.5 Evaluating Sources

While in the process of finding sources you must constantly evaluate their quality and usefulness. Conducting an Internet search on Wolfgang Amadeus Mozart, for instance, presents over 625,000 websites. Obviously it would be impossible to visit each and every site, but more importantly, not all of the sites will contain accurate or useful information. A researcher has the responsibility to seek out texts that are reliable, veracious and authoritative.

You must first decide the kind of information for which you are looking: facts, opinions, news reports, research studies, analyses, histories, personal reflections, etc. You can then narrow the likely places that such information can be found, and begin to evaluate in-depth the texts you encounter. You must be able to determine whether the book or article you are reading is a primary or secondary source. A primary source consists of the author's own work, including field research reports, laboratory studies, diaries and speeches, or other original documentation, such as legislatives bills, eyewitness accounts, and novels. A secondary source is one that comments on a primary source. Although a primary source is not always more reliable than a secondary source, it does have the advantage of being a firsthand account.

5.5.1 Evaluating Internet Sources

The Internet can provide access to many important sites and sources. For instance, you can do a search on database sites, such as JSTOR (www.jstor.org) or ProQuest Educational Journals (www.proquest.com), enabling you to read full-length articles from numerous academic journals. Any webpage you access, whether well-established or of unknown reputation, should be evaluated according to its authorship, accuracy, and the over-arching goals of the site.

All websites have an author or creator. In some cases this information is readily available, making it possible for one to do a background search of the author. This information is advantageous in order to understand better the author or web monitor's background and the possible biases he or she may have. University websites and http://www.writers.net are good places to begin when searching for academic writers. Once you have determined who the author is, you need to verify whether or not the information provided on the website is the original work of the author. Often you will find exactly the same information on a number of different sites, indicating that there is either no known original source/author, or that many sites have copied from one original, either with or without the author's consent. In your search, you should always attempt to find the original author.

Rather than having a single author, many websites are sponsored by organizations. Again, you should be aware of the group, institution or organization's background, bias, ideals, aims, etc., when evaluating the information provided. You should also be aware that some encyclopedic sites (particularly, Wikipedia) allow anyone to edit or add information and opinions. While this is useful in some instances, it also opens the door to negligence and unintentional or purposeful misinformation. At a minimum, in order for a website to remain accurate, it should be updated on a fairly regular basis. Normally, you can find the date of the latest update near the bottom of the Homepage.

In terms of accuracy, you should determine whether or not a website includes a Bibliography or Works Cited page. An academic author generally provides a detailed list of his or her bibliographic sources, and may make available links to other sites with similar or useful content. However, even academic websites are rarely peer-reviewed. That is to say, the information provided on a website contains only the opinion of the author, webmaster or creator of the site, making it difficult for the reader to obtain a balanced perspective of the information provided. It is important, therefore, that researchers seek out peer-reviewed and monitored texts – most easily found in the form of academic journals. In the latter case, articles will not only have been read and reviewed by other experts in the field, but the journals also provide an avenue for dialogue among scholars. Often you will find that an author will write a letter or article to contradict or refute the findings of another published work. By reading both articles the researcher is able to gain a more complete picture of a given topic. As mentioned, however, such academic dialogues rarely occur on websites. Therefore, it is crucial for students to look beyond the Internet for reliable, peer-reviewed texts.

Finally, one should also try to evaluate the goals of the website. In many instances an organization or author, especially an academic writer, will clearly state his or her objective in creating the website. You should, therefore, ascertain what the author or organization is trying to accomplish. Additionally, you should determine the primary target audience for the website. For instance, information about heart disease contained on a website geared toward high school aged-students will differ significantly from one providing detailed surgical procedures for a cardiologist. By understanding the target audience, one is better able to evaluate the depth and accuracy of the text.

5.5.2 Evaluating Bibliographic Citations

Evaluating a bibliographic citation, such as books, journals, and magazines, among others, is similar to evaluating Internet sources; extensive background research should always be conducted in order to fully comprehend a source. You should begin with a search of the author or organization that is taking responsibility for the publication. A writer's nationality, education, affiliations (academic and non-academic) and employment can often be identified, which may enable you to better understand the author's background and/or biases. The author's area of expertise should also be established. This can be accomplished by determining whether or not he or she has other publications, and where the publications can be found.

When reading journals or other periodicals, it is important to note whether or not the publication is monitored or peer reviewed. For instance, most magazines articles are read by an editor or editorial board before being published. However, the editor may also state that particular content or individual articles may not represent the views or opinions of the magazine as a whole. In such instances, the text is not considered peer-reviewed. On the other hand, most reputable academic journals will only accept an article once it has passed a series of peer reviews. That is, each article will be evaluated by someone other than the original author who is an expert in a similar field. Then, after revisions have been made, the article can be resubmitted for final publication. As with Internet sources, the intended audience of a book, journal, or other text, should be taken into consideration.

The publication date of the text should also be evaluated. In some fields there is a constant need to update information in order to incorporate new discoveries. However, one should not necessarily immediately dismiss a book only because it was first published decades ago. The theoretical background for some fields may have been established ten, twenty, or fifty years ago, and many of the books written seemingly a long time ago are still relevant and stand as a foundation for the field. For instance, a student may be tempted to dismiss John Blacking's book, *How Musical is Man?* because it was published in 1973. However, this book is considered one of the most important and seminal books in ethnomusicological literature.

5.5.3 Evaluating the Contents (of a book or journal)

The Table of Contents, Indices, Appendices, and entire content of a book or journal should also be examined when evaluating a source. A student may only be interested in one topic or chapter discussed in a book, but it is useful to understand how that chapter relates to others. Rarely does an author write a chapter that is completely unrelated to the entirety of his or her argument. Rather, each chapter is integral to the whole. Even if one does not intend to read the entire book in detail, at a minimum the Preface and/or Introduction should be read carefully, as it will explain the context of the work, and the role of each chapter within the integrated whole.

The bibliography, works cited, credentials, and other related materials of a book or article can also be very beneficial in expanding one's own set of sources. One author may lead you to resources with which you would otherwise be unfamiliar. This is especially true of dissertations and theses, where the graduate student must demonstrate extensive knowledge of the literature available in his or her field.

Students are taught in this book, and elsewhere, to provide a clear thesis statement when writing an essay or report; the same holds true for every good writer. Therefore, when evaluating a text, one should first look for the author's thesis or thesis statement. Then, through a thorough reading of the text, one should determine how well the author was able to substantiate his or her intended thesis. A convincing author should be able to provide facts, instead of, or at least in addition to, personal opinions and propaganda. Determining whether or not a topic is covered in a comprehensive or limited manner, as well as an objective or emotional manner is also beneficial in evaluating a text.

5.6 Becoming an Active Reader

People tend to read differently depending on the purpose or type of reading they are conducting. For instance, the reading of a novel for pleasure may allow one to be relaxed and to take time to enjoy the author's mastery of language, whereas the reading of a newspaper in the morning before rushing off to school may only provide time for a quick scan of the headlines. The latter is an example of passive reading – wherein the goal is only to receive cursory information, but not necessarily to fully process the information, or make any kind of intellectual response to it. In the process of preparing a research paper, however, you must learn to become an **active reader**. Many students are under the false impression that when preparing for a research paper he or she must follow a linear writing process: read first, think later, and write last. It is however, imperative to ask questions throughout the reading process, as well as to engage in writing as one reads.

5.6.1 Recognizing Your Reaction to a Text

A step to productive reading is to understand your own reaction to a text. You should not only ask questions of the author and the text itself, but also ask questions of yourself and your reaction to the text. As you begin to read and think actively, it becomes easier to pay more attention to the text, as well as your own reaction to it. It is advisable to keep track, via a journal or notes on a bibliography card, how the text makes you feel while you are reading it. If you find yourself getting angry, bored, interested, or excited, ask yourself why. Try to determine what the author has said and how he or she has said it that incites such a reaction in you. Pay attention to your own responses as they may be the seeds for your paper.

5.6.2 Entering the Conversation

According to Karen Gocsik of Dartmouth College, "[w]hen a writer writes a book she is, in a sense, inviting you into an ongoing conversation. She is taking a position in the great human debate, and she is asking you to take yours. When you write a paper in college, you are entering this conversation. Understand that scholarship is the written exchange of a particular community – in this case, the academic community. As a student, you have joined this community … [and] you must listen well, you must think on your feet, and you must contribute to the conversation in a way that is relevant, thoughtful, and interesting" (Dartmouth Writing Program, 2004, Coming Up With Your Topic, pp. 2-3).

In order to enter the conversation fully as a writer, you must first enter the conversation fully as a reader. As mentioned in the previous section, you must pay attention to the text and take note of how you feel about what the author is saying. Then you can go beyond your own reactions and begin asking other types of questions. For instance, if you were able to have a conversation with the author face to face, what types of questions would you would want to ask her? Are there inconsistency in text you want clarified? Are there arguments that are incomplete or lacking? Can the conclusion drawn by the author be adapted or applied to other situations? By asking these types of questions, you can begin to have a "conversation" with the author, and move beyond your own reaction to the text in order to a gain a more profound understanding of the arguments the author is making.

5.6.3 Using the Margins

As an extension to making note of your reactions to a text, one of the most important habits you should establish when becoming an active reader is the practice of making use of the margins. As has been said, an unmarked book is an unread book. Marking a text as you read, whether by underlining or by taking detailed notes in the margins, ensures that you are reading actively. Even the simple act of underlining a passage requires you to ask yourself what is most important in the text. The act of weighing importance is one way of breaking the habit of passive reading. As you underline, it is important that you look for the primary thesis of the text, or the main point of a paragraph. You need not underline an entire, lengthy passage. Rather, it is important that you seek out, and then highlight the core information that is being presented.

When marking in the margins you can do much more than simply make note of the important passages. The margins are the ideal place to ask and answer questions you may have. You are provided with space to draw arrows, establish connections, or note patterns of imagery or language in the text. If you find contradictions, you should make a reference, including the page number of the incongruous information.

♦ It should be noted, however, that when reading a book borrowed from the library, one should be courteous to the readers who will come after you. You should, therefore, either use your own copy of the text, or make your markings lightly in pencil, and erase them before returning the book. Be mindful that others may be reading for different purposes and thus will be asking different questions.

5.6.4 Moving Outside the Text

It is important to understand that every text has a context. Every writer has some aim or motivation for writing, and for writing it in a specific manner. Every writer is influenced by other writers, by his or her personal history, by the forces of his or her culture, and by the events of his or her time. If you understand the context of a text, you can better see the forces that moved the author to write that work; you will gain clarity about what and why the writer was writing. You must also take into consideration your own context. That is, your background, socio-economic circumstance, life experiences, gender, etc. As you come to understand yourself, you will come to a better understanding of your reactions to what you read.

5.6.5 Creating an Annotated Bibliography

Another important step in becoming an active reader is to create an annotated bibliography, which will enable you to recall and document properly the information you have collected throughout the reading and early writing processes, when you are ready to prepare your preliminary and final drafts. An annotated bibliography should contain the following information:

- Author and/or Editor's Name
    - Include name of translator if relevant
- Title
    - Books: complete name of book, including subtitle
    - Edited volumes: name of chapter(s) you are referencing, as well as complete title of book and editors
    - Periodicals: name of articles, as well as complete name of journal, and all other relevant information related to its publication
- Location and Name of Publisher
- Date
    - Periodicals: include, publication date, number, and volume (i.e. *Anthropological Linguistics* 25.4 (Winter 2004): 125-157.)
- Page numbers
- Source: record where you found the text (library, personal collection, governmental office, etc.)
    - Include the call number if using library sources
- Summarization of the contents
    - Arguments made by the author
    - Purpose/thesis of the text
- Paraphrases of important passages
- Notation of direct quotes
- Assessment or reflections on what you have read

There are a number of different methods for recording your annotated bibliography; you may write it out by hand or create a computer file or database. It is highly recommend that when writing the information by hand you use note cards as an organizational tool. For instance, compared to larger sheets of paper, you can easily organize or sort the note cards in an order that is most useful for you later: alphabetically, chronologically, argumentative, etc. It is also important that you remain consistent in your practice of data collection.

A thorough annotated bibliography will also help you avoid the possibility of purposefully or inadvertently plagiarizing a text. If you intend, if even think you might want to make a direct citation – that is a quote – of a particular text in your paper, then you must provide all the relevant information on your annotated bibliography note cards. On the other hand, if you want only to paraphrase the author, then your notes must indicate your own writing and your own thoughts regarding the text, by way of a summary, a set of questions and answers, or an explanation of what you have read.

In order to avoid plagiarism you must get in the habit of learning to properly paraphrase and summarize a text. It is imperative that you read and re-read the text you want to summarize and then, without consulting the original text, record in your own words your understanding of what you have read. A summary it not merely a condensing of the author's text, it should more accurately represent your understanding of and reaction to the text. You should then check your own version with the original for content, accuracy, and mistakenly borrowed phrases. Section 5.9.1 (Tips for Documenting Sources) shown below provides more practical information that will help you create a thorough and useful annotated bibliography.

5.7 Becoming an Active Writer

As mentioned above, research and writing do not have to be a linear progression from reading to thinking to writing. Rather, you should integrate the processes and begin writing as you read. As you actively read, be sure that you write down your questions to the author or about the text, and your own responses. You may also engage in a number of preliminary writing practices that will help you formulate your final paper.

5.7.1 Brainstorming

Brainstorming is a way for you to think quickly of a number of questions or definitions about a particular subject. The goal is to jot down as briefly as possible key words or phrases that come to mind as you begin pondering a topic. You can also note those things you *do not* know about the topic. At this stage, you need not concern yourself with judging the ideas themselves, or with grammatical, structural or stylistic accuracy. While it is beneficial to brainstorm at the beginning of your research process, you do not need to limit the exercise only to your initial study. Rather, any time you feel writer's block, or are having difficulty advancing to the next stage of your writing, take a moment to brainstorm the possibilities of a continued or new direction for your paper.

5.7.2 Free-writing

Free-writing is similar to brainstorming in that it is intended to be a quick and informal method of developing ideas. However, rather than creating a mere list of ideas, the goal of free-writing is to expand your thinking and to elaborate on the ideas you have already developed. Again, with this activity it is not necessary to be overly concerned with grammar or syntax. You should instead concentrate on writing in a stream of consciousness manner – putting down on paper whatever comes to mind concerning a particular idea, question or topic. Your free-writing notes can then form the foundation of your more formal first or exploratory draft.

5.7.3 Creating a Thesis Statement

As part of your initial writing, it is helpful to create a working thesis for your paper. A thesis statement is a very specific statement – it should cover only what you want to discuss in your paper, and be supported with specific evidence. The scope of your paper will be determined by the length of your paper and any other requirements that might be in place. The thesis statement, therefore, should be a concise foundation upon which the remainder of your paper will be built and generally consists of two parts: your topic, and then the analysis, explanation(s), or assertion(s) that you are making about the topic.

5.7.4 Creating an Outline and Organizing Your Notes

Once you have accomplished your preliminary brainstorming, free-writing and/or thesis creation, the next step for an active writer is to create an outline for your paper. The outline can follow the same general shape and flow of the final paper: introduction-body-conclusion. The outline serves as an aid to the process of writing and should be of the following: general description of your topic presented in a logical manner, a schematic summary, an organizational pattern, and a visual or conceptual design for your writing. In other words, an outline reflects logical thinking and clear classification while at the same time provides a visual representation of the relationships among your ideas, and serves as an ordered overview of your writing.

Most people tend to make their outlines informal. That is, you can create an organized system of only key words and phrases that convey the topics and subtopics that will be treated in your draft(s) and final paper without the constraints of proper syntax or grammar.

An outline should provide you with the following: a list of the major points of your paper, a list of subordinate points you wish to cover – listed beneath the major points, and a clear, organized depiction of the order in which your ideas are to be presented. Although an outline is only a skeleton of your paper, writing it will clarify your thinking, organize your material, and allow you to fill in the details of your final draft in an organized and effective manner. Preparing the outline may also provide you the momentum you need to start writing the final draft.

Also, if you have chosen to prepare your annotated bibliography on note cards, you will find that they can now be arranged easily to correspond with the flow of your outline. You can make notes in your outline to indicate, for instance, where you want to place a particular quote or how you wish to use the information you have gathered during the research phases.

As part of the process of creating an outline for your paper, you should also organize your notes so that you can input your collected data, including proper documentation and citation, into the first or exploratory draft. Throughout this process you should continue to do the following:

- Analyze, synthesize, sort, and digest the data you have collected;

- Narrow your sources to those that can most easily and effectively be included in your draft and final paper;
- Verify any and all data you have collected; and
- Communicate clearly your own thoughts, insights, and ideas in relation to your data.

5.8 Creating an Exploratory Draft

If you have followed the general process outlined above, much of your work will have already been completed by the time you write your first draft. During the research and preliminary writing stages, you should have already determined your prospective audience, and molded your work accordingly. As you prepare your draft you must, therefore, keep in mind the needs and expectations of your audience.

The exploratory draft and the final paper follow the same pattern as an academic essay except on a much larger or more expanded scale. Therefore, you should refer to Chapter Five for writing and organizational ideas. Just as you must explore your own methods of conducting research, writing is a very personal activity: there is no single, correct way to write a research paper. In some instances you may want to begin with the introduction. You will have already created a thesis statement, thus you may want to begin your draft by placing that statement in a broader context. At other times you may want to begin with the body of your paper. You may, for instance, begin writing about topics with which you are most familiar, allowing you to ease into the more difficult or troubling passages of your research.

What is important is that you write! This seems like an obvious statement, but often students become flustered or overwhelmed when they are faced with the task of writing a lengthy paper. Remember, if you develop the habit of becoming an active reader and writer, the creation of a preliminary draft will be much easier. Another principle that may be helpful is to get in the habit of writing everyday. At times you may think you are experiencing writer's block. However, if you will make a goal of writing for at least ten to fifteen minutes a day, or writing just one paragraph everyday, you will find that the writing process becomes much easier and more enjoyable. Some days you may in fact only produce a single sentence or paragraph, one that you may even discard later, but having determined to write on a daily basis, you will find that other days are far more productive. If you try to complete the research and writing of a substantial paper the night before it is due, you (and your audience) will likely be very disappointed in the results, and you will have missed an opportunity not only to fulfill the requirements for a course, but more importantly to become truly edified.

Throughout the entire research and writing process there are two essential components that you must constantly be aware of and be diligent in fulfilling: avoid plagiarism and make sure your own voice is clearly heard in your writing.

5.9 Plagiarism and the Misuse of Sources

Plagiarism has always been a concern for teachers and students alike. However, the advent of digital technology and the use of the Internet have only served to exacerbate the concerns, suspicions, and consequences of plagiarism. In short, plagiarism occurs when a writer uses someone else's ideas, words, information, art work, charts, diagrams, etc. without properly citing the original source. Distinctions can be made between **deliberate plagiarism** (buying, stealing or borrowing a paper, or hiring someone to write a paper for you), **misuse of sources** (carelessly or inadequately citing ideas or words borrowed from a source), and possible **accidental or unintentional plagiarism** (using a source too closely when paraphrasing or building on someone else's idea without proper citation). However, no matter where one falls in the spectrum of plagiarism, it remains a serious problem that can result in severe punishment, including expulsion from school. Although in some cultures the proper documentation of sources is not taken as seriously as in others, in the US and the UK, and by extension in International Studies programs throughout the world, plagiarism is of grave concern and must be avoided at all costs.

As mentioned above, depending on one's educational background, some students may simply be unaware of proper documentation requirements and procedures, while others may be more deliberate in their attempt to pass off someone else's work as their own. There are several factors that may lead a student to plagiarize: fear of failure or thinking one's own work will not be as good as that of others; poor time-management skills and failure to plan in advance for the necessary time it takes to prepare a research paper; or viewing a course, assignment, conventions of academic documentation, or consequences of cheating as unimportant.

Although a student may feel justified in his or her use undocumented sources, the fact remains that plagiarism, in any form, is a serious matter and all effort should be made to avoid it. If a man were intending to have a tumor removed from his brain, he would no doubt hope that his surgeon would have actually completed her own research and study of the brain, rather than cheating and copying from someone else's work, merely because the competition in medical school was fierce. Although this is an extreme example, the principle remains the same. In the end, there is no benefit in plagiarizing.

If all one does is learn to copy the words and ideas of others, one will have failed to truly learn and think for oneself. At some point in life, you must be accountable for what you know directly, not merely what you can read from someone else. If you follow the research and writing pattern suggested above, there will be little chance of plagiarism, as you will have devoted the necessary amount of time to the research process, and will have properly documented all resources. Below are some suggestions to help you create an effective annotated bibliography and develop habits, which, if properly applied, will enable one to avoid plagiarism.

5.9.1 Tips for Documenting Sources

In the following instances you must fully **document** your sources:

- Direct quotes, paraphrases or use in any way of someone else's words or ideas, including from print (books, magazines, journals, newspapers, etc.), electronic sources (web sites, television, video, radio, computer programs, etc.) or any other medium.
- Any information that was gained through a personal interview, whether conducted by you or someone else.
- Ideas that were obtained from any type of correspondence, including letters, emails, and telephone conversations.
- The use of any exact words or phrase that is unique to someone else.
- The use of someone else's documents, art work, charts, diagrams, illustrations or pictures (including anything from an Internet source).

If any of the following circumstances exist, there is **no need to document** a source:

- The information provided regards your own experiences, observations, ideas, insights or conclusions.
- The information compiled includes generally well known facts.
- The information you are discussing is accepted as "common knowledge," including proverbs or axioms, folklore, or common sense observations.
- Your writing is based on your own experiments or field research.

The following suggestions, adapted from Purdue's Online Writing Lab, are also beneficial in providing a means to ensure that all of your work – both in the research and writing processes are properly documented. Notice that each category is subdivided into two sections: actions that should be taken during the research and writing process; and the appearance of the quote or paraphrase in one's final document.

1. When researching, note-taking, and interviewing

Action during the writing process:

- Mark *everything* that is someone else's words with large quotation marks (perhaps in a second color) or with a big **Q** (for **quote**).
- Indicate in your notes those ideas that are taken from sources (**S**), compared to those ideas that are your own insights (**ME**).
- As mentioned in Section 5.6.5 (Create an Annotated Bibliography), record all of the relevant documentation

information in your notes.

Appearance on the finished product:

- Your final paper should clearly indicate, via one of the following methods anything that is taken from a source other than yourself. The final draft should be thoroughly proofread and checked in order to verify accuracy.
    - In-text citation
    - Footnotes
    - Bibliography
    - Quotation marks
    - Indirect quotations

2. When paraphrasing and summarizing

Action during the writing process:

- First, write your paraphrase and summary without looking at the original text, so you rely only on your memory.
- Next, check your version with the original for content, accuracy, and mistakenly borrowed phrases.

Appearance on the finished product:

- Begin your summary with a statement giving credit to the original source: According to Bob Dylan…
- Put any unique words or phrases that you cannot change, or do not want to change, in quotation marks: …"savage inequalities" exist throughout our educational system (Kozol).

3. When quoting directly

Action during the writing process:

- Make sure the author's name is near the quote and clearly

marked in your notes, and in your paper.

- Select direct quotes that make the most impact in your paper – too many direct quotes may lessen your credibility and interfere with your style. See Section 5.8.2 (Letting Your Own Voice be Heard) below.

Appearance on the finished product:

- Mention the person's name either at the beginning of the quote, in the middle, or at the end.
- Put quotation marks around the text that you are quoting, unless you have a long, block quote.
- Indicate any changes to the original (the addition or omission of a capital letter) or added words and phrases in brackets ([ ]) and omitted text with ellipses (. . .).

4. When quoting indirectly

Action during the writing process:

- Keep the person's name near the text in your notes, and in your paper.
- Rewrite the key ideas using different words and sentence structures than the original text.

Appearance on the finished product:

- Mention the person's name either at the beginning of the information, or in the middle, or at that end.
- Double check to make sure that your words and sentence structures are different than the original text.

Good research, documentation and writing are all part of the learning process. It is essential, therefore, that as you begin any new project you keep these guidelines in mind. In the end, your arguments, thesis and entire paper will be stronger and more convincing if you learn to be wise in your use of sources. Chapter 6 in this volume will discuss stylistic choices and specific systems for the proper citation of quotes and paraphrases, summaries and bibliographies.

5.9.2 Letting Your Own Voice Be Heard

Although a research paper does in fact need to contain the results of your research, as evidenced through direct quotes, summaries, or the paraphrasing of others' work, it is also important that your own voice, your ideas, your musings, your results from field work, and your conclusions be clearly and distinctively heard in your paper. Many students want to prove how much research they have done by using numerous quotes. However, if you have done your research properly, you will always have read, studied, and absorbed a great deal more information than could possibly be shared in a single paper. Your objective should be to integrate smoothly the ideas of others into your own thinking. Gordon Harvey of Harvard College proposes three guiding principles when incorporating sources into your paper (1998:3-5, emphasis in original):

1. *Use sources as concisely as possible, so your own thinking isn't crowded out by your presentation of other people's thinking, or your own voice by your quoting other voices.* This means you should summarize your source unless you have a good reason to paraphrase closely or quote more extensively.

2. *Never leave your reader in doubt as to when you are speaking*

and when you are using material from a source. Avoid the ambiguity by citing the source immediately after drawing on it, but also (if discussing the sources or quoting it directly) by announcing the source in your own sentence or phrase preceding its appearance, and by following up its appearance with commentary about it or development from it that makes clear where your contribution starts. . . .

3. *Always make clear how each source you introduce into your paper relates to your argument.* This means indicating to the reader, in words leading up to your summary, paraphrase, or quotation of a source, or in the sentences that follow and reflect on it (or in both), what you want the reader to notice of focus on in the quote.

Your own arguments and voice can certainly be enhanced and strengthened by the proper inclusion of other's work, but do not be afraid to make a stance through or own words. Use quotations sparingly, allowing your own conclusions to be the ones the reader comes away contemplating.

5.10 Revisions, Rewriting and Preparation of the Final Draft

By this point in the research and writing process, the majority of the work is behind you. However, the final steps in creating a finished product are as important as the proceeding ones. First, as discussed above, in order to avoid plagiarism and the misuse of sources (or even the appearance thereof) you should check and recheck all of your documentation and citations. Second, you should revise and rewrite your original draft. Mozart was a gifted composer, who, it would appear from his musical sketches, did very little editing of his pieces and was apparently able to write a complete score with very few errors or changes. Beethoven, on the other hand, continually worked, and reworked, wrote and rewrote his pieces. His sketch books reflect a mind that was rarely satisfied with his initial creations. Sometimes he would jot down only a simple phrase or melody, later indicating one or two or more possibilities of how that tune could be realized in a harmonic context. Sometimes it was not until years later that his ideas were fully developed and incorporated into a symphony, concerto, or other large work.

Although there are some "Mozarts" in the academic and writing worlds, most of us are have much more in common with Beethoven. Therefore, when planning, researching, and writing an extensive paper, prepare well and take ample time to complete your task. If your teacher gives you the greater portion of a semester to write a research paper, then you should use the entirety of those two or three months to create a quality paper. Many students feel overwhelmed, are prone to procrastination, or feel they have too much other work to accomplish during the course of a semester to concentrate on a paper that will not be due for months to come. However, if you begin the research and writing in a timely manner, then the process will not only be more pleasant and fruitful, but more importantly, the final product will be far superior. If the research paper process is approached correctly, the result may be beneficial not only to the writer, reader and one's colleagues, but may also lead to the creation of a publishable piece of writing.

The final step in creating a masterful research paper, which is often overlooked or done in haste, is proofreading. All writers make mistakes, but all writers must also make a concerted effort to correct as many of the mistakes as possible. Many writers (and sadly, many editors, too) rely heavily on word processors and spell check programs to detect their errors. Although these tools can be of use, they must not replace the process of proofreading by the author herself, and if possible by a colleague or other outside readers. Once you have worked on a project for a long time, you are often unable to see mistakes that readily stand out to a set of fresh eyes. Because you will have completed your writing a day or two before the paper is actually due, you should have time to solicit the help of a classmate in reading your paper, while you can do the same for them. The outside proofreader can help point out not only grammatical or spelling errors, but also illogical sequences, incomplete citations, or lack of proper conclusions, as well as comment on brilliant and persuasive writing.

5.11 Conclusion

Learning to write a thorough and convincing research paper takes a great deal of practice. Some students have had opportunities throughout their early education to prepare such a paper. However, it may not be until college that others begin the task of completing their first major research and writing activities. Regardless of your background, with proper planning, productive allocation of time, the building of good research and writing habits, including becoming an active reader and writer, you can learn to produce papers of superior quality. You must find what methods of study work best for you, often through trial and error, but in time and with practice you can become a successful academic writer.

References

Berke, Jaqueline and Randal Woodland. 1994. *Twenty Questions for the Writer: A Rhetoric with Readings*, 6th ed. Boston: Heinle.

Christensen, Dieter. n.d. Personal Communication.

Dartmouth Writing Program. Karen Gocsik. 2004. *Writing the Academic Paper: Coming Up With Your Topic*. <http://www.dartmouth.edu/~writing/materials/student/ac_paper/topic.shtml>. Accessed: August 4, 2005.

Harvey, Gordon. 1998. *Writing with Sources: A Guide for Students, Indianapolis*. Indiana: Hackett Publishing Company.

Pearsall, Thomas E., and Donald H. Cunningham. 1988. *The Fundamentals of Good Writing*. New York: Macmillan Publishing Company.

Purdue University Online Writing Lab. 1995-2003. <http://owl.english.purdue.edu/> Accessed: August 4, 2005.

Chapter 6 Documenting Sources and Works Cited

6.1 Introduction

Nearly every academic discipline has its own preferred editorial style for formatting, documenting and citing sources and for listing the works that have been cited. This book, for instance, uses the American Political Science Review (APSR) system. An instructor may request that students use a particular system, or students may at times be able to choose for themselves. In either case, it is important for students to choose one system, and follow all of the rules of that system consistently throughout his or her paper – including in-text citations and the bibliography or works cited section, as well as for over-all formatting.

The primary elements of a bibliographic reference are the same for most styles of documentation, although the order in which they are presented may vary. These elements include the name of the author, the title, the place of publication, the publisher's name, the date of publication, and a designation of the location, or page number of a reference. For electronic sources, however, some elements may be missing or must be adapted from the information that is available. For example, in place of an author's name, online webmasters or monitors may only use login names or aliases. Instead of a title, there may only be a file name. The place of publication and the name of the publisher are replaced by the online protocol and address. Rather than a date of publication, the date you access the site may be the only means of designating the specific "edition" of an online work. Additionally, on the World Wide Web, a given site is always one page, regardless of its actual length. Thus, alternative means to pagination must be provided so that a reference is complete, and that the reader can access the same information as the writer.

In this chapter, the three most popular systems used among professors of International Studies will be introduced and compared: APSR, APA (American Psychological Association), and ASA (American Sociological Association). Although the Chicago and MLA (Modern Language Association) styles are also very popular among many scholars, they will not be covered in this chapter. Except for a brief discussion about footnotes and endnotes, formatting issues will also not be discussed in this chapter. The in-text citation standards of each system will be presented followed by a comparison of the relevant bibliography or works cited notation systems. Except where noted, examples are taken from Heather Willoughby's dissertation, *The Sound of Han: P'ansori, Timbre, and a South Korean Discourse of Sorrow and Lament.*

What is presented herein will likely not address every situation you may encounter. Additionally, in the section on references, many of the citation methods may look similar, however, there are often subtle differences, including the number of spaces required after a period, or the use of single or double spacing. It is advisable, therefore, in prepare your document you first consult the style manual, or visit the appropriate official website of each association.

Like Chapter 2, this chapter is essentially a reference chapter. You may refer to specific sections when you are required to produce a piece of work that conforms to one of the systems of formatting, documenting and citing sources discussed in detail. Alternatively, you may refer to some of the examples presented to double-check that you are covering all the information required in a full citation. You do not need to read it straight through, as you will only be using one of the systems presented at any one time, and may conceivably be using an entirely different system (although it will nevertheless contain many similar elements).

Please note, that double spacing is generally required for all type-written or computer generated essays and research papers. For convenience, most examples are single spaced in this chapter, except for block quotes, which are shown as they should appear in your document. When preparing your document, all quotes and citations should follow the double space standard, except in the case of some block quotes that are single spaced, as demonstrated below.

6.2 In-text Citations

As the name indicates, in-text citations are references to other people's ideas and words, whether paraphrased, summarized, or quoted within the context of your paper. They are designed to provide the reader with only a cursory amount of critical information without interrupting the flow of argument. A brief, parenthetical citation usually contains the author's last name and the page number of the reference or the author's last name, the date of publication, and the page number of the reference. This practice is also sometimes referred to as an embedded citation. Often, for electronic sources, some or all of these elements may be missing. Thus, parenthetical references to electronic sources will usually include only an author's last name or, if no author's name is available, the file name, and if possible, the date of publication or the date of access if no publication date is available. The following sections will discuss the standard in-text citation standards for the most commonly encountered types of texts. For references not found herein, please refer to the style manual associated with the system you are using.

6.2.1 APSR

APSR is the standard citation system for most political science publications, including publications in Korea such as *International Studies Review*. Citations should be made in your paper as close to the reference as possible, so as to avoid any confusion about whose ideas are being expressed. In the APSR system, a citation usually includes only the last name of the author(s), the year of publication and the page number(s) in parentheses. Be sure that every cited work is included in the reference section and that the spellings of the authors' names and dates of publications are accurate in both citations and references.

- **Direct Quotes** If the name of the author appears before the quote, then only the date and page are cited in parentheses. If the author's name is not mentioned, it too is added to the parenthetical citation, as in the following examples. Notice carefully the placement of punctuation (commas, quotation marks and periods).

  As Foucault succinctly concludes, "discourses … [are] … practices that systematically form the objects of which they speak" (1972, 49).

  "Music, as an aesthetic practice articulates in *itself* an understanding of both group relations and individuality, on the basis of which ethical codes and social ideologies are understood" (Frith 1996, 110).

- **Paraphrases or Summaries** Reference the author(s) in the text, followed by a parenthetical citation with date and page of source.
  Lila Abu-Lughod and Catherine Lutz (1990, 9-10) contend that emotional discourses situated in every talk are not so much a reflection of a society's experience, but are constitutive of a reality that is understood by the social participant.

- **Block Quotes** If a quote is five lines or longer, it should be placed in the text as a block quote. The entire quote is indented equally for both the left and right margins. Block quotes should be single spaced. You do not use quotation marks with block quotes and the citation is place at the end of the quote, with the final punctuation after the citation, as in the following example:

  > As the kwangdae strives to reflect the everyday life and so mirror the realities of his [sic] listener's lives, the suffering and lamentations of the characters are frequently less in service of the plot than of the audience's need for catharsis. Although, in some p'ansori plots, distress and suffering lead eventually to a happy result, the process of suffering itself seems more important to the audience than the happy outcome. . . . P'ansori distinguishes itself as a popular literature by eliciting sympathy through suffering: it give its audience a means to endure sorrow (Pihl 1994, 5-6).

- **More than One Work Cited in a Summary** All sources should be listed with author date, page (if applicable) – separated by a semi-colon, as in the following example:

  In fact, South Korea's recorded histories are replete with

attempts to build a national culture by emphasizing the supposed homogeneity of the people… (Cho 1987; Eckert 1990; Abelmann1996).

Citations:

1) **Single Author**

(Williams 1977, 17)

a) **Single Author with More than One Publication in the Same Year** add consecutive letters to the year

(Song 1983c)

2) **Two Authors**

(Feld and Fox, 1994)

a) **Authors with the Same Last Name** add first initials to distinguish between the authors:

(I.H. Kim 1979, 32; J.U. Kim 1991, 57)

3) **Three or More Authors** cite all names the first time and the first author followed by "et al." in subsequent citations:

First citation:

(Fairbank, Reischauer, and Craig 1989, chs. 1 and 5)

Subsequent citations:

(Fairbank, et al. 1989, 12)

4) **Unknown Author** If no author or editor is given, start the citation with the title of the source. Then, list the item in the bibliography or works cited section according to the title's first word (not including a, an, or the), as in the following example:

In-text:

(The Korea Herald 2005, 16).

Bibliography:

"Baez performs for Crawford war protesters." 2005. *The Korean Herald*, 23August, A16.

5) **Government, Institution, or Organization as Author** Details on government documents should be in the reference section. For citations in the text, the name of the source, date, and page number in parentheses suffice. Citations to all other public documents may use the standard form identified in an opening note.

(Congressional Record September 20, 1977, H6)

(Senate Foreign Relations Committee Print January 10, 1980, 24)

(Papers of President Ronald Reagan February 23, 1981, 10)

(National Center for Korean Traditional Performing Arts 2005)

6) **Indirect Sources** If you are citing a source that was originally found within another source, you should make note of both in your in-text citation, and include both sources in your bibliography or works cited.

"This film makes us aware of our homeplace (*kohyang*) and through p'ansori shows us the beauty of *han* which is at the center of our (national) emotions" (Yi 1993, 84 as cited in Koh 1995, 3).

7) **Electronic Sources** Citations for information found on the World Wide Web, an e-mail message, an electronic mailing service (listserv message) or other electronic forms should follow the common in text pattern of author, year and, if available, the page number. If the electronic source does not have page numbers, it is appropriate to use internal divisions such as section numbers or chapter headings to assist the reader in finding the original information.

(CIA 1999, Afghanistan/Government)

This is the only information available regarding APSR in-text citations of electronic sources. However, there are often many other types of sources than are covered here. Therefore, you should consult the other systems and adapt them as necessary to APSR standards.

8) Other

a) Historical Citations

i) The reference section should refer the reader to the current source for a historical work:

(Freud 1961, ch. 2)

(Hamilton, Madison, and Jay 1960, 456-462)

i) Citations to classical authors such as Thucydides, Aristotle, and Plato may use standard forms identified in an opening note:

I cite Thucydides according to the standard form: book, paragraph and, when necessary, sentence (e.g., 3.46.2); unless otherwise noted, all the translations are my own. I cite Plato according to the standard Stephanus pagination; I have used Bloom's translation, Plato (1968).

b) Legal Sources Legal citations include the case name, year, and page number if warranted:

(Baker v. Carr 1962, 190)

More complete citations belong in the reference section. (If possible, use the U.S. Reports for Supreme Court decisions; this source is preferable to the Lawyers' Edition or Supreme Court Reporter.)

c) Repeated Citations Repeat citation each time it is necessary. Avoid "ibid.," "op. cit.," or "supra."

6.2.2 APA

Many social science classes and publications advocate the use of APA for citations. The following information is based on the *Publication Manual of the American Psychological Association,* 5th ed. (Washington: APA, 2001). As with the APSR examples, most are taken from Dr. Willoughby's dissertation, except in the case of the "Electronic Sources," which are based on the work of Diana Hacker.

- **Direct Quote** Introduce the quotation with a signal phrase, that is, a short phrase that indicates you will be inserting the words of another author (e.g. Jimmy Dean says…; As McEnroe concludes…; Dr. Livingston presumed…). The signal phrase includes the author's last name followed by the date of publication in parentheses. Put the page number (preceded by "p.") in parentheses after the quotation. If the signal phrase does not name the author, include the author's last name with the year and the page number in parentheses after the quotation. Use commas between items in the parentheses.
  As Foucault (1972) succinctly concludes, "discourses … [are] … practices that systematically form the objects of which they speak" (p. 49).
  "Music, as an aesthetic practice articulates in *itself* an understanding of both group relations and individuality, on the basis of which ethical codes and social ideologies are understood" (Frith, 1996, p. 110).

- **Paraphrases or Summaries** The author's last name and the date should be included either in a signal phrase introducing the material or in parentheses following it. Although a page number is not required for a summary or a paraphrase, include one if it would help readers find the passage in a long work.

Lila Abu-Lughod and Catherine Lutz (1990) contend that emotional discourses situated in every talk are not so much a reflection of a society's experience, but are constitutive of a reality that is understood by the social participant.

(or)

Researches contend that emotional discourses situated in every talk are not so much a reflection of a society's experience, but are constitutive of a reality that is understood by the social participant (Abu-Lughod and Lutz, 1990, p. 9-10).

- **Block Quotes** For quotations longer than forty words, indent each line one-half inch, or five spaces, from the left margin, but do not justify the right margin. Double space between the body of the paper and the quotation, and double space the quotation. Quotation marks are not needed for block quotes, as in the following example:

> As the kwangdae strives to reflect the everyday life and so mirror the realities of his [sic] listener's lives, the suffering and lamentations of the characters are frequently less in service of the plot than of the audience's need for catharsis. Although, in some p'ansori plots, distress and suffering lead eventually to a happy result, the process of suffering itself seems more important to the audience than the happy outcome. . . . P'ansori distinguishes itself as a popular literature by eliciting sympathy through suffering: it give its audience a means to endure sorrow (Pihl, 1994, p. 5-6).

- **More than One Work Cited in a Summary** When your parenthetical citation includes two or more works, put them in the same order that they appear in the bibliography, separated by semicolons.

In fact, South Korea's recorded histories are replete with attempts to build a national culture by emphasizing the supposed homogeneity of the people… (Abelmann, 1996; Cho, 1987; Eckert, 1990).

Citations

1) **Single Author**

(Williams, 1977, p. 17)

a) **Single Author with More than One Publication in the Same Year** When your list of references includes more than one work by the same author in the same year, use lowercase letters ("a," "b," and so on) with the year to order the entries in the reference list. Use those same letters with the year in the citation.

(Song 1983c)

2) **Two Authors** Name both authors in the signal phrase or parentheses each time you cite the work. In the parentheses, use "&" between the authors' names; in the signal phrase, use "and."

Feld and Fox (1994) cite numerous recent ethnographies in support of their claim that sound reflects social structure and that musical performance embodies and articulates social imagination and practices (p. 38).

(or)

Sound reflects social structure and musical performance embodies and articulates social imagination and practices (Feld & Fox, 1994, p. 38).

a) **Authors with the Same Last Name** To avoid confusion, use initials with the last names if your reference list

includes two or more authors with the same last name.
Research by I.H. Kim (1979) revealed that . . .
Researchers have found that . . . (I.H. Kim, 1979, 32; J.U. Kim 1991, 57).

3) **Three or More Authors** Identify all authors in the signal phrase or parentheses the first time you cite the source. In subsequent citations, use the first author's name followed by "et al" (without a comma or period in between) in either the signal phrase or the parentheses.
First citation:
(Fairbank, Reischauer, & Craig, 1989).
Subsequent citations:
(Fairbank et al., 1989).
   a) **Six or More Authors** Use only the first author's name followed by "et al." in the signal phrase or the parentheses.
   (Savage-Rumbaugh et al., 1993).
4) **Unknown Author** If the author is unknown, mention the work's title in the signal phrase or give the first word or two of the title in quotation marks, followed by a comma in the parenthetical citation. Titles of articles and chapters are put in quotation marks; titles of books and reports are italicized.
("Baez performs," 2005.)
   a) In the rare case when "Anonymous" is specified as the author, treat it as if it were a real name: (Anonymous, 2001). In the list of references, also use the name Anonymous as author.
5) **Government, Institution, or Organization as Author** Name the organization, institution or governmental agency in the signal phrase or in the parenthetical citation the first time you cite the source. If the organization has a familiar abbreviation, you may include it in brackets the first time you cite the

source and use the abbreviation alone in later citations.
First citation:
(National Center for Korean Traditional Performing Arts [NCKTPA], 2005)
Subsequent citations:
(NCKTPA, 2005)

6) **Indirect Sources** If you use a source that was cited in another source (a secondary source), name the original source in your signal phrase. List the secondary source in your reference list and include it in your parenthetical citation, preceded by the words "as cited in." In the following example, Koh is the secondary source.
Yi commented that, "This film makes us aware of our homeplace (*kohyang*) and through p'ansori shows us the beauty of *han* which is at the center of our (national) emotions" (as cited in Koh, 1995, p. 3).

7) **Electronic Sources** Where possible, an electronic document should be documented in a manner similar to other documents (using the author-date style). However, many electronic sources lack the authors' names, dates, or other pertinent information, such as page numbers. In addition, they may lack page numbers (required in some citations). Suggestions are presented below for dealing with such situations according to APA style guidelines.
   a) **Known Author**
   R. Fouts and D. Fouts (1999) have explained one benefit of ape language research: It has shown us how to teach children with linguistic disabilities.
   b) **Unknown Author** If no author is named, mention the title of the document or provide the first word or two of the title in parentheses:

According to a BBC article, chimpanzees at sites in West Africa, Tanzania, and Uganda exhibit culture-specific patterns of behavior when grooming one another ("Chimps," 1999).

c) **Unknown Date** When the date is unknown, use the abbreviation "n.d." (for "no date").

   Attempts to return sign-language-using apes to the wild have had mixed results (Smith, n.d.).

d) **Unknown Page Number** Ordinarily, page numbers are required for direct quotations, and where applicable for paraphrases and summaries as well. When an electronic source lacks numbered pages, your citation should include – if possible – information that will help readers locate the particular passage being cited. When an electronic document has numbered paragraphs, use the paragraph number preceded by the symbol ¶ or by the abbreviation "para."

   (Hall, 2001, ¶5)

   (or)

   (Hall, 2001, para. 5).

e) **Known Author, Unknown Page and Paragraph Number** If you know the author, but neither a page nor a paragraph number is given and the document contains headings, cite the appropriate heading and indicate to which paragraph you are referring:

   According to Kirby (1999), some critics have accused activists in the Great Ape Project of "exaggerating the supposed similarities of the apes [to humans] to stop their use in experiments" (Shared Path section, para. 6).

f) Electronic files using portable document format (PDF) often have real page numbers. In such instances, provide the page number in the parenthetical citation.

6.2.3 ASA

ASA is the preferred style for documents relating to or published in sociological journals, and is likewise used in some international studies reports and research papers. Romelia Salinas and the University of Vermont, Department of Sociology were consulted for the ASA style guidelines.

- **Direct Quotes** When an author's name appears in the text it should be followed by the publication year in parentheses. However, if an author's name is not in the text, enclose the last name and publication year in parentheses (with no comma). Pagination follows year of publication after a colon (with no space between the colon and page number). Quotations in the text begin and end with quotation marks. The author, date, and page numbers follow the end-quote and precede the period.
  As Foucault (1972) succinctly concludes, "discourses … [are] … practices that systematically form the objects of which they speak" (p. 49).
  "Music, as an aesthetic practice articulates in *itself* an understanding of both group relations and individuality, on the basis of which ethical codes and social ideologies are understood" (Frith 1996:110).

- **Paraphrases or Summaries** As with direct quotes, if the author's name appears in the text it should be followed by the publication year in parentheses. If an author's name is not in the text, enclose the last name and publication year in parentheses (with no comma).

Lila Abu-Lughod and Catherine Lutz (1990) contend that emotional discourses situated in every talk are not so much a reflection of a society's experience, but are constitutive of a reality that is understood by the social participant.
(or)
Researches contend that emotional discourses situated in every talk are not so much a reflection of a society's experience, but are constitutive of a reality that is understood by the social participant (Abu-Lughod and Lutz 1990:9-10).

- **Block Quotes** Present block quotations in a separate, indented paragraph without quotation marks. The quote should be double spaced. The author, date, and page number follows the period in a block quote. In the block quote below, notice that a period follows the end of the quote, then the parenthetical citation contains a "P" for page that is capitalized because the author and date have already been mentioned. Additionally, there is no period after the parentheses.
As Pihl (1994) has noted:

> As the kwangdae strives to reflect the everyday life and so mirror the realities of his [sic] listener's lives, the suffering and lamentations of the characters are frequently less in service of the plot than of the audience's need for catharsis. Although, in some p'ansori plots, distress and suffering lead eventually to a happy result, the process of suffering itself seems more important to the audience than the happy outcome. . . . P'ansori distinguishes itself as a popular literature by eliciting sympathy through suffering: it give its audience a means to endure sorrow. (P. 5-6)

- **More than One Work Cited in a Summary** A series of references should be separated with semicolons. You can either list the references alphabetically or chronologically, but you must remain consistent throughout the paper.
  In fact, South Korea's recorded histories are replete with attempts to build a national culture by emphasizing the supposed homogeneity of the people… (Cho, 1987; Eckert, 1990; Abelmann, 1996).

Citations

1) **Single Author** The following information is included in parentheses: author's name (no comma) publication year (colon, no space) page number.
   (Williams 1977:17)
   a) **Single Author with More than One Publication in the Same Year** When your list of references includes more than one work by the same author in the same year, use lowercase letters ("a," "b," and so on) with the year to order the entries in the reference list. Use those same letters with the year in the citation.
      (Song 1983c)
2) **Two Authors** Give both names for two joint authors in the following manner:
   Feld and Fox (1994) cite numerous recent ethnographies in support of their claim that sound reflects social structure and that musical performance embodies and articulates social imagination and practices (P. 38).
   (or)
   Sound reflects social structure and musical performance embodies and articulates social imagination and practices (Feld and Fox 1994:38).

3) **Three Authors** If a work has three authors, cite all three last names in the first citation; thereafter, use "et al." in the citation. Notice there is no comma after the last name or et al. preceding the date.
   First citation:
   (Fairbank, Reischauer, and Craig 1989).
   Subsequent citations:
   (Fairbank et al. 1989).
   a) **Four or More Authors** If the work has more than three authors, use *et al.* in the first citation as well as in all subsequent citations. Notice that in this case the *et al.* is in italics with no comma before the date.
      (Savage-Rumbaugh *et al.* 1993).
4) **Unknown Author** If the author is unknown, give the work a short title, based on the first word or two of the original title in quotation marks, followed by the date (with no comma in between).
   ("Baez performs" 2005.)
5) **Government, Institution, or Organization as Author** For institutional, organizational or governmental authorship, supply minimum identification from the beginning of the complete citation.
   First citation:
   (National Center for Korean Traditional Performing Arts [NCKTPA] 2005)
   Subsequent citations:
   (NCKTPA 2005)
6) **Electronic Sources** Examples provided by the University of Vermont, Department of Sociology.
   a) For web sites, follow the following format:
      American Sociological Association. 1997. "Call for Help:

Social Science Knowledge on Race, Racism, and Race Relations" (ASA Action Alert, October 15). Washington, DC: American Sociological Association. Retrieved October 15, 1997 (http://www.asanet.org/racecall.htm).

b) For electronic journals, follow the following format:
Smith, Herman W. and Takako Nomi. 2000. "Religiosity and Life Satisfaction across the Life Course." Social Indicators Research 48:3. Retrieved January 19, 2001 (http://www.wkap.nl/issuetoc.htm/0303-8300+48+3+1999).

c) For full text databases, follow the following format:
Garcia, Alma M. 1998. "An Intellectual Odyssey: Chicana/Chicano Studies Moving into the Twenty-first Century." Journal of American Ethnic History 18:109-114. Retrieved January 19, 2001 (http://infotrac.galegroup.com/itweb/utexas_main).

6.3 Bibliography, References, and Works Cited

As with in-text citation and formatting issues, each system also dictates its own rules for bibliographies and works cited pages. The following provides a guide for the most commonly used types of sources. Although the systems may look very similar, there are subtle differences regarding punctuation and spacing between words and punctuation. It is advisable that you refer to the respective style manuals to resolve any question you may have, or to clarify the reference practices for types of works not covered in this chapter. Topics not coved in this chapter that can be found in the style manuals include: personal communications, biblical references, works in an anthology, multivolume works, letters to the editor, reviews, CD-ROM abstracts, dissertations and theses, proceedings of a conference, computer programs, and other types of media, such as videos, television, and radio programs.

It should be noted that there is a slight difference between a bibliography and references or works cited. In a bibliography, all texts, whether print or electronic, that you refer to directly, or that you consulted in your research can be listed. However, in the case of references or works cited pages, *only* those references that you directly quote, paraphrase, summarize or otherwise refer to in your paper are listed. In other words, all references cited in the text must be in the reference list, and vice versa.

Regardless of the style or reference system you choose to employ, make sure that your margins are left justified for the bibliography; otherwise you will not be able to provide the correct spacing. In the following example, the first is left justified, whereas the latter is center justified: notice the difference in the spacing, particularly how there are unnatural spaces in the second example.

Cain, A., & Burris, M. (1999, April). Investigation of the use of mobile phones while driving. Retrieved January 15, 2000, from http://www.cutr.eng.usf.edu/its/mobile_phone_text.htm

Cain, A., & Burris, M. (1999, April). Investigation of the use of mobile phones while driving. Retrieved January 15, 2000, from http://www.cutr.eng.usf.edu/its/mobile_phone_text.htm

General Guidelines

APSR All references are double-spaced, and all lines after the first in an entry are indented. References are listed alphabetically by author. When several works by the same author are listed, they should appear in chronological order, with the earliest publication first. Two or more works by the same author in the same year should be listed alphabetically by title. In the parentheses, following the year, add "a," "b," and so on. Use these same letters when giving the year in the in-text citation. If no date is provided, use "nd" (both lower case letters, no periods).

APA The first line of an entry is placed at the left margin with all subsequent lines indented ½ inch (or five spaces). Double spacing is used throughout. References should be listed alphabetically by author. If more than one reference is listed for the same author, the authors full name is written for each entry; they should be listed chronologically with the earliest reference first. Two or more works by the same author in the same year should be listed alphabetically by title. In the parentheses, following the year, add "a," "b," and so on. Use these same letters when giving the year in the in-text citation. If no date is provided, use "n.d." (both lower case letters, with period after each). Italicize the titles and subtitles of books; capitalize only the first word of the title and subtitle (and all proper nouns). Capitalize names of periodicals as you would capitalize them normally.

ASA Indent all lines after the first by ½ inch, and double space all entries. List authors alphabetically. If the same author has two or more citations with the same year, distinguish them with lowercase letters following the date. If the same author is listed for more than one reference, the authors name should be replaced with six hyphens and a period (------.) in the later citations. Note however, that if the latter reference is co-authored, both authors' names must appear in full. If no date is available, use "N.d." (upper case "N" lower case "d" with periods). Except for New York City, US Postal Code abbreviations must be included for all state names, even if the city is well known (e.g. Chicago, IL), country names are also added if reference is from outside the US (e.g. London, England).

1. Book with One Author

APSR

Kendall, Laurel. 1988. *The Life and Hard Times of a Korean Shaman*. Honolulu: University of Hawaii Press.

Kendall, Laurel. 1996. *Getting Married in Korea: of Gender, Morality and Modernity*. Berkeley: University of California Press.

Kendall, Laurel and Mark Peterson, eds. 1983. *View from the Inner Room*. New Haven, CT: East Rock Press.

APA Notice the date is in parentheses. Notice also that only the first word in the title, the first word of the subtitle and proper nouns are capitalized.

Kendall, L. (1988). *The life and hard times of a Korean shaman*. Honolulu: University of Hawaii Press.

Kendall, L. (1996). *Getting married in Korea: Of gender, morality and modernity*. Berkeley: University of California Press.

Kendall, L. & M. Peterson. (Eds.). 1983. *View from the inner room*. New Haven, CT: East Rock Press.

ASA

Kendall, Laurel. 1988. *The Life and Hard Times of a Korean Shaman*. Honolulu, HI: University of Hawaii Press.

------. 1996. *Getting Married in Korea: of Gender, Morality and Modernity*. Berkeley, CA: University of California Press.

Kendall, Laurel and Mark Peterson, eds. 1983. *View from the Inner Room*. New Haven, CT: East Rock Press.

2. Later Editions of Books

APSR

Feld, Steve. 1990. *Sound and Sentiment: Birds, Weeping, Poetics and Song in Kaluli Expression*, 2nd ed. Philadelphia: University of Pennsylvania Press.

APA

Feld, S. (1990). *Sound and sentiment: Birds, weeping, poetics and song in Kaluli expression* (2nd ed.). Philadelphia: University of Pennsylvania Press.

ASA

Feld, Steve. 1990. *Sound and Sentiment: Birds, Weeping, Poetics and Song in Kaluli Expression.* 2nd edition. Philadelphia, PA: University of Pennsylvania Press.

3. Reprint Editions

APSR The date of the earlier edition is placed in brackets [ ] before the more recent edition.

Underwood, Lillias Horton. [1904] 1987. *Fifteen Years Among the Top-Knots*. Seoul: Royal Asiatic Society, Korean Branch.

APA No period after (Original work published 1904)

Underwood, L. H. (1987). *Fifteen years among the top-knots*. Seoul: Royal Asiatic Society, Korean Branch. (Original work published 1904)

ASA Earlier edition is placed in brackets [ ] before the more recent edition.

Underwood, Lillias Horton. [1904] 1987. *Fifteen Years Among the Top-Knots*. Seoul, Korea: Royal Asiatic Society, Korean Branch.

4. Translations

APSR Notice that there are two different methods for citing translations according to APSR. In the second, the original publication date is added.

Bakhtin, Mikail Mikhailovich. 1981. *The Dialogic Imagination*, trans. Caryl Emerson and Michael Holquist. Austin: University of Texas Press.

(or)

Bakhtin, Mikail Mikhailovich. 1981. *The Dialogic Imagination*, trans. Caryl Emerson and Michael Holquist. Austin: University of Texas Press. (Original work published in 1975).

APA

Bakhtin, M. M. (1981). *The dialogic imagination* (Caryl Emerson and Michael Holquist, Trans.). Austin: University of Texas Press.

ASA

Bakhtin, Mikail Mikhailovich. 1981. *The Dialogic Imagination*. Translated by Caryl Emerson and Michael Holquist. Austin, TX: University of Texas Press.

5. Books with Two or More Authors

APSR With two or more authors or editors, only the first author is listed family name first. Authors should be listed in the order found in the source material rather than alphabetically. Notice the comma after the second name.

Fairbank, John, Edwin Reischauer, and Albert Craig. 1989. *East Asia: Tradition and Transformation*. Boston: Houghton Mifflin.

APA All author's names are listed family name first (comma), followed by his or her given name initial(s) and a comma.

Fairbank, J., Reischauer E., & Craig, A. (1989). *East Asia: Tradition and transformation*. Boston: Houghton Mifflin.

ASA Only the first author's name is written family name first.

Fairbank, John, Edwin Reischauer, and Albert Craig. 1989. *East Asia: Tradition and Transformation*. Boston, MA: Houghton Mifflin.

6. Government, Institution, or Organization as Author

APSR

The National Center for Korean Traditional Performing Arts. 2005. *Pansori: Commemorating Designation as a Masterpiece of Oral Tradition and Intangible Heritage of Humanity by UNESCO in 2003*. Seoul: The National Center for Korean Traditional Performing Arts.

U.S. Congress, Senate Committee on Foreign Relations. April 1984. *Report on Covert Aid to Central America*. 98th Cong., 2nd sess. Washington: Government Printing Office.

APA If the publisher is the author, write the word "Author" as the publisher. If the report has an author, begin with the author's name, and name the publisher at the end.

The National Center for Korean Traditional Performing Arts. (2005). *Pansori: Commemorating designation as a masterpiece of oral tradition and intangible heritage of humanity by UNESCO in*

2003. Seoul: Author.

U.S. Congress, Senate Committee on Foreign Relations. (April 1984). *Report on covert aid to Central America.* 98th Cong., 2nd sess. Washington, DC: U.S. Government Printing Office.

ASA

The National Center for Korean Traditional Performing Arts. 2005. *Pansori: Commemorating Designation as a Masterpiece of Oral Tradition and Intangible Heritage of Humanity by UNESCO in 2003.* Seoul, Korea: The National Center for Korean Traditional Performing Arts.

U.S. Congress, Senate Committee on Foreign Relations. April 1984. *Report on Covert Aid to Central America.* 98th Congress, 2nd session. Washington, DC: Government Printing Office.

7. Unknown Author

APSR If no author or editor is given, your in-text citation should include the title of the source, year and page (The Korean Herald 2005, 16). Then, list the item in your bibliography or works cited according to the title's first word (not including a, an, or the).

"Baez Performs for Crawford War Protesters." 2005. *The Korean Herald*, 23August: A4.

APA Begin the reference with the work's title. Titles of books are italicized. Titles of articles are neither italicized nor put in quotation marks.

Baez performs for Crawford war protesters. (2005, August 23). *The Korean Herald*, p. A4.

ASA Two different citations methods were found for this

situation.

"Baez Performs for Crawford War Protesters." 2005. *The Korean Herald*, August 23,

p. 4.

(or)

Unknown Author. 2005. "Baez Performs for Crawford War Protesters." *The Korean Herald*, August 23, p. 4.

8. Edited Volumes

APSR Note that you rarely cite an edited book unless you are referring to arguments made in the whole volume. Use "ed." if there is one editor, or "eds." if there are more than one.

Abu-Lughod, Lila and Catherine A. Lutz, eds. 1990. *Language and the Politics of Emotion*. Cambridge: University of Cambridge Press.

APA In parentheses, use "Ed." for a single editor, or "Eds." for more than one.

Abu-Lughod, L. & Lutz, C.A. (Eds.). (1990). *Language and the Politics of Emotion*. Cambridge: University of Cambridge Press.

ASA

Abu-Lughod, Lila and Catherine A. Lutz, editors. 1990. *Language and the Politics of Emotion*. Cambridge, England: University of Cambridge Press.

9. Chapter or Article in an Edited Volume

APSR You should include the book chapter's pages from the beginning of the article to the end (Pp.). Note that editors are listed first name-family name, in the order listed in the source rather than alphabetically. If the chapter and volume editor are the same, repeat the name, as in the first example.

Abu-Lughod, Lila and Catherine A. Lutz. 1990. "Introduction: Emotion, Discourse and the Politics of Everyday Life." In *Language and the Politics of Emotion*, eds. Lila Abu-Lughod and Catherine A. Lutz. Cambridge: University of Cambridge Press. Pp. 1-22.

Christensen, Dieter. 1991. "Traditional Music, Nationalism, and Musicological Research." In *Music in the Dialogue of Cultures: Traditional Music and Cultural Politics*, ed. Max Peter Baumann. Berlin: Florian Noetzel Verlag Wilhelmshaven. Pp. 215-223.

APA Begin the reference with the author, year of publication, and title of the article or chapter (with no quotation marks). Then write "In" and give the editor's name, followed by "Ed." in parentheses; the title of the book; and the page numbers of the article or chapter in parentheses. End with the book's publication information.

Abu-Lughod, L. & Lutz, C.A. (1990). Introduction: Emotion, discourse and the politics of everyday life. In L. Abu-Lughod & C.A. Lutz (Eds.), *Language and the Politics of Emotion* (pp. 1-22). Cambridge: University of Cambridge Press.

Christensen, D. (1991). Traditional music, nationalism, and musicological research. In M.P. Baumann (Ed.), *Music in the dialogue of cultures: Traditional Music and Cultural Politics* (pp. 215-223). Berlin: Florian Noetzel Verlag Wilhelmshaven.

ASA As with other citations, the author's name is followed by the date. The title of the chapter (in quotation marks) is followed by the pages ("Pp."), the word "in" (without capitalization), the title of the book in italics, and finally "edited by."

Abu-Lughod, Lila and Catherine A. Lutz. 1990. "Introduction: Emotion, Discourse and the Politics of Everyday Life." Pp. 1-22 in *Language and the Politics of Emotion*, edited by Lila Abu-Lughod and Catherine A. Lutz. Cambridge, England: University of Cambridge Press.

Christensen, Dieter. 1991. "Traditional Music, Nationalism, and Musicological Research." Pp. 215-223 in *Music in the Dialogue of Cultures: Traditional Music and Cultural Politics*, edited by Max Peter Baumann. Berlin, Germany: Florian Noetzel Verlag Wilhelmshaven.

10. Journal/Periodicals Articles with One Author

APSR In the first example, 21 is the volume number and 2 is the issue. Sometimes the issue will be indicated by a month (e.g. February), which should, like 2 in this case, be placed in parentheses. In the second example, there is no issue, therefore, only the volume is mentioned.

Jairazbhoy, Nazir. 1977. "The 'Objective' and Subjective View in Musical Transcription." *Ethnomusicology* 21 (2): 263-73.

Willoughby, Heather. 2000. "The Sound of *Han*: *P'ansori*, Timbre and a Korean Ethos of Pain and Suffering." *Yearbook for Traditional Music* 32: 17-30.

APA In the first example the title of the journal is in italics followed by a comma and the volume, also in italics. The issue number is in plain text in parentheses, followed by a comma and page numbers.

Jairazbhoy, N. (1977). The 'objective' and subjective view in musical transcription. *Ethnomusicology, 21* (2), 263-273.

Willoughby, H. (2000). The sound of *han*: *P'ansori*, timbre and a

Korean ethos of pain and suffering. *Yearbook for Traditional Music 32*, 17-30.

ASA The format for ASA journals is similar to that of APSR, however, there are no spaces between the volume, issue number, colon, and page numbers.

Jairazbhoy, Nazir. 1977. "The 'Objective' and Subjective View in Musical Transcription." *Ethnomusicology* 21(2):263-73.

Willoughby, Heather. 2000. "The Sound of *Han*: *P'ansori*, Timbre and a Korean Ethos of Pain and Suffering." *Yearbook for Traditional Music* 32:17-30.

11. Journal/Periodical Articles with Two or More Authors

APSR

Feld, Steven and Aaron Fox. 1994. "Music and Language." *Annual Review of Anthropology* 23: 25-53.

APA

Feld, S. & Fox, A. (1994). Music and language. *Annual Review of Anthropology, 23*, 25-53.

ASA

Feld, Steven and Aaron Fox. 1994. "Music and Language." *Annual Review of Anthropology* 23:25-53.

12. Newspapers with Known Author (for unknown authors, refer to number 7 above)

APSR

Vinograd, Cassandra. 2005. "Humans Are Ones on Display at

London Zoo." *Springfield News-Sun*. 26 August: B2, B12.

APA

Vinograd, C. (2005, August 26). Humans are ones on display at London Zoo. *Springfield News-Sun*, pp. B2, B12.

ASA

Vinograd, Cassandra. 2005. "Humans Are Ones on Display at London Zoo." *Springfield News-Sun*, 26 August, B2, B12.

13. Magazines, Known and Unknown Author

APSR Use "np" for "no page number," as in the second reference.

Harris, Richard. 2005. "Expats Unlock the Mysteries of Korea." *Morning Calm*, July: 48-57.

"Madam Poison." 2005. *Harper's Bazaar*, February: np.

APA Use "n.p." for "no page number," as in the second example.

Harris, R. (2005, July). Expats unlock the mysteries of Korea. *Morning Calm*, 48-57.

"Madam Poison." (2005, February). *Harper's Bazaar*, n.p.

ASA Use "N.p." for "no page number," as in the second example.

Harris, Richard. 2005. "Expats Unlock the Mysteries of Korea. *Morning Calm*, July, pp. 48-57.

"Madam Poison." 2005. *Harper's Bazaar*, February, N.p.

(or)

Unknown Author. 2005. "Madam Poison." *Harper's Bazaar*, February, N.p.

Electronic Sources

Electronic sources vary greatly as to the amount of information they provide regarding author, date, and pages numbers. When referencing electronic sources, it is difficult to always provide the information that would normally be required for printed matter. The most important thing to remember, therefore, is to provide as much information as possible so that the reader can easily retrieve the same "text." The following three suggestions are applicable to all reference styles:

- Avoid dividing an electronic address at the end of a line. If absolutely necessary, divide it at a slash (/) or before or after a period.
- Cite web items that refer to specific Web site documents rather than to home or menu pages.
- Provide accurate addresses (URLs) so that the reader can find the "text" to which you are referring. Continually check your references to Web documents; if the addresses of any document you are using changes, update your references before you submit your paper.

In this section, only the most common electronic sources will be discussed. You should consult the respective style manual you are using for further details. Additionally, there are many useful websites that provide electronic sources reference guides. A few will be listed at the end of this chapter in the references. Examples for electronic sources are provided by the following: Bruce Drury and Mark Seltzer (APSR); Mary Ellen Guffey and Diana Hacker (APA); and Romelia Salinas and Big Bend Community College (ASA).

14. Information Posted on Websites

APSR The reference listing for a WWW citation should contain the author's name; date of publication or last revision; title of document; title of complete work (if provided), underlined; URL, in angled brackets; and date of access, in parentheses. In the first two examples, there is a known author. In the third example, there is no known author or date provided on the website.

Central Intelligence Agency. 1999. Afghanistan/Government. World Fact Book, 1998. <html://www.odci.gov.cia/publications /factbook/af.html> Accessed: January 29, 1999.

Economist. "The King is Dead, Long Live the King." 2002. Economist, 22 December, 15-18. <http://www.lclark.edu/ ~msetzler/PolSysLC/CPSf2002readingsbank/ econKing.html>. Accessed: April 10, 2003.

Citizens for Fair Elections. ND. Elections Outcomes. <http:// www.elections.org/artcles/no_author.html>. Boston: Citizens for Fair Elections. June 20, 2001.

APA Provide as many of the following details as possible: author's name, date of publication (if there is no date, use "n.d."), title of document (in italics), date you accessed the source, and a URL that will take readers directly to the source. In the first example, the source has both an author and a date. If a source has no author, begin with the title and follow it with the date in parentheses (if available), as in the second example. The third example was retrieved from a university program's Web site; therefore, the name of the program should be included in your retrieval statement.

Cain, A., & Burris, M. (1999, April). Investigation of the use of mobile phones while driving. Retrieved January 15, 2000, from http://www.cutr.eng.usf.edu/its/mobile_phone_text.htm

Exploring nonverbal communication. n.d. Retrieved July 8, 2001, from http://zzyx.ucsc.edu/~archer

Cosmides, L., & Tooby, J. (1997). Evolutionary psychology: A primer. Retrieved July 5, 2001, from the University of California, Santa Barbara, Center for Evolutionary Psychology Web site: http://www.psych.ucsb.edu/research/cep/primer.html

ASA The first example is from a professional or organizational website, while the latter is from a personal website.

American Sociological Association. 2000. "Scholarship of Teaching and Learning Workshop." Washington, DC: American Sociological Association, Retrieved May 5, 2000 (http://www.asanet.org/members/socwkshp.html).

Joseph Pellegrino. 1999. "Homepage." Retrieved May 31, 2001 (http://www.english.eku.edu/pellegrino/default.htm)

15. Magazine or Journal Articles from a Database

Many universities provide access to databases, which in turn give you access to electronic versions of articles from magazines and journals. Popular databases include: JSTOR, EBSCO, ProQuest, among many others.

APSR If you are citing an article from an electronic database and both the original publication data and original pagination are available, cite the article as you would if you found it in the original source. If you do not have the original pagination, give as much data about the original article as you can, and then note the electronic source (JSTOR or Academic Elite, as in the example that follows) and the date of access.

Carter, Heather A. and Robert L. Jones. 1995. "The Article Title."

Journal Title 55 (February): 112-142. EBSCO Host Academic Elite, June 31, 2002.

APA Include as much of the following information as possible, with accurate punctuation: Author(s). (Date). Title. *Magazine or Journal Title, volume* (issue), paging. Retrieved [date], from [database], Article No. (if given).

Blackburn-Brockman, E. & Belanger, K. (2001, January). One page or two? A national study of CPA recruiters' preferences for resume length. *The Journal of Business Communication, 38* (1), 29. Retrieved February 28, 2003, from InfoTrac College Edition database, Article No. A71327300.

If the article is from a journal or magazine that is only found on the Internet, include the following: Author(s). (Date). Title. *Magazine or Journal Title, volume* (issue), page number (if given). Retrieved [access date] from [URL]

Whetstone, J.T. (2002). Civility and the cell phone: What would George Washington say? *Electronic Journal of Business Ethics and Organization Studies, 7*(1). Retrieved March 3, 2003, from http://ejbo.jyu.fi/index.cgi?page=articles/0701_6

ASA As with the other systems, include all the information from the original sources, as well as a reference to the database from which you retrieved the text (in this case, ProQuest Direct).

Roberts, Leslie. 1999. "It's alive! (or might be) The science and ethics of creating life in a lab." U.S. News & World Report, 127:24 (1 page). Retrieved May 17, 2001 Available: ProQuest Direct (http://proquest.umi.com/pqdweb).

16. Emails and Distribution Lists

APSR Provide the author's name, the author's email address (in angled brackets), the date of publication, the subject line from posting, the type of communication (personal email, distribution list) in square brackets, and the date of access (in parentheses).

Albright, M. <albright@state.gov> 1999, Jan.5. Statement on Cuba [Personal email]. (1999, January 29)

APA E-mail messages may be cited in the text, but APA warns against listing them in the "References" section because such messages are unrecoverable by others.

6.4 Footnotes and Endnotes

As you will have noticed, APSR, APA, and ASA all prefer the use of in-text citations. Other systems, most notably the Chicago style, call instead for the use of footnote citations. In such cases, citations are made in the text by placing a superscript number after each quotation, paraphrase, or summary. Citations are numbered sequentially throughout the text, and each citation corresponds to a numbered note containing publication information about the source cited. Such notes are called *footnotes* when printed at the foot of a page and *endnotes* when printed at the end of an essay, chapter, or book. These notes generally serve two purposes: to cite sources and to make cross-references to previous notes.

Footnotes or endnotes of another variety are often required within your research paper, and particularly when submitting an article for publication in a journal. Footnotes contain explanations of material that is pertinent to your topic, but which are either too lengthy to be included in the text itself, or would be distracting to the flow of the paragraph. Many times a footnote or endnote will clarify or elaborate either on an outside source or on the opinions of other authors.

Every publication has its own standard and rules for the inclusion of footnotes. Therefore, if you are submitting an article for publication, you should ascertain whether or not footnotes and/or endnotes are acceptable, and the style in which they must be presented. For instance, some publications prefer footnotes that are single-spaced and use a 10-point font, while other publications require the footnotes to be double-spaced and use a12-point font, as with the remainder of the text. Others still, discourage the use of footnotes all together, but may allow for endnotes. As with other formatting issues, you should consult the relevant style manual and/or publication guidelines for further details regarding the use of footnotes and endnotes.

6.5 Summary

All systems of citation, including those covered in this chapter (APSR, APA, and ASA) have very specific rules regarding in-text and bibliographic citations. However, each system also provides guidelines about the ways in which the page should be formatted or about the use of footnotes and endnotes; such topics were not addressed in this chapter. Remember to consult the style manual of the system you are using in order to ensure that all of your formatting is in accordance with the requisite specification. The following include some of the important aspects of a paper that should be taken into consideration when preparing your document: footnotes or endnotes; margins, spacing, and indentations; page numbering; title page; punctuation; abstracts; headings and subheadings; visuals (including figures, tables, and appendices); and abbreviations.

References

American Psychological Association. 2001. *Publication Manual of the American Psychological Association,* 5th ed. Washington, DC: American Psychological Association.

Big Bend Community College. 2002, *Source of Your Information (ASA Style).* <http://cmsalpha.bbcc.ctc.edu/soc/refs/source_of_information_ASA.htm>. Accessed: August 27, 2005.

Drury, Bruce. [1992] 1999. *American Political Science Association Style Manual.* <http://dept.lamar.edu/polisci/DRURY/drury.html>. Accessed: August 27, 2005.

Guffey, Mary Ellen. [1997] 1998-2005. *APA Style Electronic Formats.* <http://www.westwords.com/guffey/apa.html>. Accessed: August 27, 2005.

Hacker, Diana. ND. *Social Sciences: Documenting Sources.* <http://www.calstatela.edu/library/bi/rsalina/asa.styleguide.html>. Accessed: August 27, 2005.

Salinas, Romelia. ND. *ASA Format.* <http://www.calstatela.edu/library/bi/rsalina/asa.styleguide.html>. Accessed: August 27, 2005.

Seltzer, Mark. 2000-2005. *Citation Requirements and Examples Using the American Political Science Review Format.* <http://www.highpoint.edu/~msetzler/generalissues/APSRcitation.htm#APSR%20%20Citation%20Styles%20for%20Common%20Sources>. Accessed: August 27, 2005.

Scribe, Abel. 2004. *APA Style Sheet.* <http://www.docstyles.com/archive/apacrib.pdf>. Accessed: August 27, 2005.

University of Vermont, Department of Sociology. 2002. *Department of Sociology Citation Guide.* <http://www.uvm.edu/~soceval/?Page=program/policies/citationguide.html>. Accessed: August 27, 2005.

Willoughby, Heather Alane. 2002. *The Sound of Han: P'ansori, Timbre, and a South Korean Discourse of Sorrow and Lament.* Ph.D. Dissertation. Department of Music, Columbia University, New York, NY.

Appendix

There are several Romanization systems used by academics to transliterate Korean names and words. The most well-known and widely used are the McCune-Reischauer (McC-R) system and the 2000 Revised Romanization of Korean (R) system used by the Korean Government. When preparing a paper that includes Korean terms, you should choose to use one or the other Romanization system, and assure that you are consistent and thorough in your transliterations. Exceptions include names that are already established by an individual or well-known business (e.g. Hyundai, Ewha). For example, 이승만 should be Romanized as Yi Sûng-man (McC-R) or Yi Seungman (R), but is commonly written as Syngman Rhee.

In your text, all Korean words that have been Romanized should be written in *italics*. Exceptions include personal names, names of cities, governmental offices, businesses, other proper nouns, or Korean words that are well known outside of Korea (e.g. kimchi).

The following chart, adapted from Stefan Ewing, depicts the Romanization for all Korean consonants and vowels. After the chart a number of examples are provided.

General rules of Romanization in the chart below include:

- "Initial" means a consonant at the beginning of a word or after a consonant. McCune-Reischauer distinguishes between initial and non-initial consonants.

- "Medial" indicates consonants that fall between vowels or after a vowel and before the consonant ㅇ.
- "Final" means at the end of a word or before a consonant (other than ㅇ). Both McCune-Reischauer and Revised Romanization distinguish between final and non-final consonants. The pronunciation of final consonants is defined by the final consonant rule, which assimilates all final consonants to one of seven permissible sounds: "k" (ㄱ), "n" (ㄴ), "l" (ㄹ), "m" (ㅁ), "b" (ㅂ), "t" (ㅅ), and "ng" (ㅇ).

Consonants

Hangul -- Consonants	McCune-Reischauer			2000 Revised	
	Initial	**Medial**	**Final**	**Initial/ Medial**	**Final**
ㄱ	k	g	k	g	k
ㄲ	kk	kk	k	kk	k
ㄳ	—	ks	k	kss	k
ㄴ	n	n	n	n	n
ㄵ	—	nj	n	nj	n
ㄶ	—	n	n	n	n
ㄷ	t	d	t	d	t
ㄸ	tt	tt	t	tt	t
ㄹ	r	r	l	r	l
ㄺ	—	lg	k, l[†]	lg	k, l

[†] Normally pronounced "k" but is instead pronounced "l" when followed by "k,"as in 맑고 (pronounced "말꼬").

ㄻ	—	lm	m	lm	m
ㄼ	—	lb	l, p[‡]	lb	l, p
ㄽ	—	ls	l	lss	l
ㄾ	—	lt’	l	lt	l
ㄿ	—	lp’	p	lp	p
ㅀ	—	r	l	r	l
ㅁ	m	m	m	m	m
ㅂ	p	b	p	b	p
ㅃ	pp	pp	p	pp	p
ㅄ	—	ps	p	pss	p
ㅅ	s	s	t	s	t
ㅆ	ss	ss	t	ss	t
ㅇ	—	ng[§]	ng	ng	ng
ㅈ	ch	j	t	j	t
ㅉ	tch	tch	t	jj	t
ㅊ	ch’	ch’	t	ch	t
ㅋ	k’	k’	k	k	k
ㅌ	t’	t’	t	t	t
ㅍ	p’	p’	p	p	p
ㅎ	h	h[**]	h	h	h

[‡] Normally “l,” but pronounced “p” for the verbs 밟다, 넓죽하다, and 넓둥글다.

[§] Normally “l,” but pronounced “p” for the verbs 밟다, 넓죽하다, and 넓둥글다.

[**] Normally not shown in the medial position.

Vowels

Hangul – Vowels	McCune-Reischauer	2000 Revised
ㅏ	a	a
ㅐ	ae	ae
ㅑ	ya	ya
ㅒ	yae	yae
ㅓ	ô	eo
ㅔ	e	e
ㅕ	yô	yeo
ㅖ	ye	ye
ㅗ	o	o
ㅘ	wa	wa
ㅙ	wae	wae
ㅚ	oe	oe
ㅛ	yo	yo
ㅜ	u	u
ㅝ	wô	wo
ㅞ	we	we
ㅟ	wi	wi
ㅠ	yu	yu
ㅡ	û	eu
ㅢ	ûi	ui
ㅣ	i	i

The McCune-Reischauer system makes note of the following irregularities:

1. ㄹ is written *r* before ㅎ.
2. ㄹ is written *n* after ㄱ, ㅁ, ㅂ, and ㅇ.

3. No letter is written for ㅇ when in the initial position (e.g. 아 = a).
4. ㄴ is written *l* before or after ㄹ.
5. ㄱ, ㄷ, and ㅂ are written *ng*, *n,* and *m* respectively before ㄴ, ㄹ and ㅁ.
6. ㅎ before ㄱ, ㄷ, ㅈ is written as an apostrophe after the initial.

There are other irregularities as well, but this list covers the most common ones, and others will be addressed in the examples below.

Consonant Clusters

The following two tables represent consonant cluster – that is, the Romanization techniques for final consonants followed by an initial consonant. For example, in the word 한문 the "ㄴ" of 한 is the final followed by the initial "ㅁ" of 문. Thus, the chart below indicates that the letters be written "nm" (hanmun). The tables only deal with the most common consonants. In some cases, when the final position consonant of one syllable is followed by the first position consonant of the next syllable, a sound change occurs. Such sound changes are highlighted in the tables. For example, in 독립, the "ㄱ" of 독 changes to "ng" and the "ㄹ" of 립 changes to "n," resulting in "tongnip" (not toklip).

McCune-Reischauer

Initial / Final		ㅇ	ㄱ	ㄴ	ㄷ	ㄹ	ㅁ	ㅂ	ㅅ	ㅈ	ㅊ	ㅋ	ㅌ	ㅍ	ㅎ
			k	n	t	(r)	m	p	s	ch	ch’	k’	t’	p’	h
ㄱ	k	g	kk	ngn	kt	ngn	ngm	kp	ks	kch	kch’	kk’	kt’	kp’	kh
ㄴ	n	n	n’g	nn	nd	ll	nm	nb	ns	nj	nch’	nk’	nt’	np’	rh
ㄹ	l	r	lg	ll	lt	ll	lm	lb	ls	lch	lch’	lk’	lt’	lp’	rh
ㅁ	m	m	mg	mn	md	mn	mm	mb	ms	mj	mch’	mk’	mt’	mp’	mh
ㅂ	p	b	pk	mn	pt	mn	mm	pp	ps	pch	pch’	pk’	pt’	pp’	ph
ㅇ	ng	ng	ngg	ngn	ngd	ngn	ngm	ngb	ngs	ngj	ngch’	ngk’	ngt’	ngp’	ngh

2000 Revised Romanization

Initial / Final		ㅇ	ㄱ	ㄴ	ㄷ	ㄹ	ㅁ	ㅂ	ㅅ	ㅈ	ㅊ	ㅋ	ㅌ	ㅍ	ㅎ
			g	n	d	r	m	b	s	j	ch	k	t	p	h
ㄱ	k	g	kg	ngn	kd	ngn	ngm	kb	ks	kj	kch	kk	kt	kp	kh(k)
ㄴ	n	n	ng	nn	nd	ll(nn)	nm	nb	ns	nj	nch	nk	nt	np	nh
ㄹ	l	r	lg	ll	ld	ll	lm	lb	ls	lj	lch	lk	lt	lp	lh
ㅁ	m	m	mg	mn	md	mn	mm	mb	ms	mj	mch	mk	mt	mp	mh
ㅂ	p	b	pk	mn	pd	mn	mm	pb	ps	pj	pch	pk	pt	pp	ph(p)
ㅇ	ng	ng	ngg	ngn	ngd	ngn	ngm	ngb	ngs	ngj	ngch	ngk	ngt	ngp	ngh

Examples

The Revised system does not always take into account the possibility of certain consonant clusters where sound changes take place in the spoken language. Although these examples are uncommon, they do occasionally occur. The author has maintained the practice of writing the Romanization according to the rules of the Revised system, despite the sound changes. These examples are marked with an asterisk (*).

Hangul – Examples	McCune-Reischauer	Revised
(ㄱ) 강산	kangsan	gangsan
독일	Togil	Dogil
국립	kungnip	gungnip
낙심	naksim	naksim
떡	ttôk	ttoek
합계	hapkye	hapgye
물건	mulgôn	mulgeon
(ㄴ) 낙랑	Nangnang	Nangnang
날	nal	nal
연락	yôllak	yeollak
한문	hanmun	hanmun
년감	yôn'gam	nyeongam
작년	changnyôn	jangnyeon
원남	Wôllam (or) Wônnam	Weollam (or) Weonnam
(ㄷ) 달	tal	dal
하다	hada	hada
삼등	samdûng	samdeung
반내다	pannaeda	bannaeda
발달	paltal	baldal
받고	patko	badgo
합동	haptong	hapdong
(ㄹ) 로	No	Lo
나라	nara	nara
실학	Sirhak	Silhak
일간	ilgan	ilgan
밀림	millim	millim
신라	Silla	Silla
함락	hamnak	hamnak
독립	tongnip	dongnip
가을	kaûl	kaeul
(ㅁ) 문	mun	mun

Hangul – Examples	McCune-Reischauer	Revised
음식	ûmsik	eumsik
사람	saram	saram
(ㅂ) 불	pul	bul
보배	pobae	bobae
동북	tongbuk	dongbuk
십명	simmyông	sinmyeong
답장	tapchang	dapjang
밥	pap	bap
(ㅅ) 사전	sajôn	sajeon
가사	kasa	kasa
울산	Ulsan	Ulsan
잣나비	channabi	jatnabi*
못하다	mothada	mothada*
옛날	yennal	yennal
웃통	utt'ong	uttong
봇	pôt	beot
(ㅇ) 알	al	al
문안	munan	munan
합의	hapûi	habui
영원	yôngwôn	yeongwon
선생	sônsaeng	seonsaeng
(ㅈ) 종	chong	jong
사정	sachông	sajeong
감자	kamja	gamja
발전	palchôn	baljeon
맞다	matta	matta
젖니	chônni	jeonni
(ㅊ) 차	ch'a	cha
가치	kach'i	gachi
꽂	kkot	kkot
(ㅋ) 큰	k'ûn	keun

Hangul – Examples	McCune-Reischauer	Revised
유쾌	yuk'wae	yukwae
부엌	puôk	bueok
(ㅌ) 타결	t'agyôl	tagyeol
검토	kômt'o	keomto
같이	kach'i	gachi
밭	pat	bat
(ㅍ) 포병	p'obyông	pobyeong
부평	Pup'yông	Bupyeong
선풍	sônp'ung	seonpung
갚니	kamni	gapni*
덮다	tôpta	deopda
(ㅎ) 형상	hyôngsang	hyeongsang
마한	Mahan	Mahan
(ㄲ) 꼭지	kkokchi	kkokji
닦는	tangnûn	dangneun
섞어	sôkkô	seokkeo
(ㄸ) 뛰다	ttwida	ttwida
어떤	ôttôn	eotteon
번뜻	pônttût	beontteut
(ㅃ) 뿌리	ppuri	ppuri
기쁜	kippûn	gippeun
(ㅆ) 쓰다	ssûda	sseuda
아저씨	ajôssi	ajeossi
있는	innûn	yinneun
섰다	sôtta	seotda
(ㅉ) 짜다	tchada	jjada
어찌	ôtchi	eojji
신짝	sintchak	sinjjak

Korean Names, Words, and Titles in Citations and References

Style manuals for citations and references (as discussed in Chapter 6) do not specifically stipulate how to deal with Korean words or titles. In general, however, practice dictates that for any Korean reference you provide a Romanized version of the Korean title, the original Korean title (in 한글), and a translation of the title. Names of Korean authors should be written as published by the author. However, some scholars will also add a transliteration of the author's name according the McCune-Reischauer or 2000 Revised Romanization, as in the second example.

Kim, Chin-yông and Kim Hyôn-ju. 1996. *Ch'unhyang-ga: Myôngch'ang Chang Cha-baek ch'angpon* 춘향가: 名唱 張子伯 唱本 (The Song of Ch'unhyang: The Singing Style of Master Singer Chang Cha-baek). Seoul: Tosôch'ulp'an Pakichông.

Han, Myong-hee [Han Myông-hûi]. 1994. *Uri karak, Uri Munhwa* 우리가락 우리문화 (Our Rhythm, Our Culture). Seoul: Ttabibat.

References

Ewing, Stefan. 2005. *21st Century Seonbi.* <http://21cseonbi.blogspot.com/2005/05/comparing-romanizations.html#6>. Accessed August 29, 2005.

McCune, G.M. and E.O. Reischauer. 1939. "The Romanization of the Korean Language: Based on its Phonetic Structure." *Transactions of the Korea Branch of the Royal Asiatic Society*, Volume XXIX. Seoul, Korea: Royal Asiatic Society.

Ministry of Culture and Tourism. 2001. *The Revised Romanization of Korea*. Seoul: Ministry of Culture and Tourism Republic of Korea. <http://www.mct.go.kr:8080/english/K_about/Language04.html>. Accessed: August 29, 2005.